THE
FREEDOM
OF
FALCONRY

S.J. MANARIN

L.R. Price Publications Ltd

S.J. MANARIN

THE FREEDOM OF FALCONRY

First published in Great Britain by
L.R. Price Publications Ltd, 2018

This edition published by
L.R. Price Publications Ltd, 2019
27 Old Gloucester Street,
London, WC1N 3AX
www.lrpricepublications.com

ISBN13 : 978-1-9164679-0-3
ISBN10 : 1916467903

DEDICATION

"To all of my friends and family who have
supported me through this journey."

S.J. MANARIN

THE
FREEDOM
OF
FALCONRY

S.J. MANARIN

S.J. MANARIN

PROLOGUE

"I don't believe it - there's a buzzard sitting on that fence!"

This excited cry came from my dad, as we were en-route to Devon, as part of our annual family holiday. I was about eight years old at the time. Being a very sensible man my dad decided to pull over and reverse on the hard shoulder of the M5 motorway so that we could once again be parallel with the magnificent bird of prey.

Perched on a post, about twenty feet above us, where the field at the side of the motorway gave way to a gate, was a medium-sized, brown raptor. I pressed my face towards the back window, and this beautiful bird turned its head to face to me.

"You can tell we're getting closer to Devon now - they only live in the West Country," my dad said.

I think the buzzard was lost on my mum - she was too preoccupied that, not only had we stopped the journey, but we had actually reversed, in the opposite direction to other vehicles, currently hurtling down the motorway at over 70mph.

The sight of the bird was not lost on me; I'm sure everyone has that one moment, when they are inspired or want to learn more about a subject - this was mine.

My dad had often taken me to bird-watching hotspots around Blakeney in Norfolk and, as impressive as the flocks of waders were, as they danced around the mud-flats, it was the sighting of a bird of prey which really took our excitement to the next level.

Seeing the marsh-harriers, soaring effortlessly on V-shaped wings, or the dive of a kestrel, after it had been hovering over its doomed snack for long enough, were some of the highlights in my memory bank - they are still as vivid today as they were in that moment, on the side of the motorway.

Sadly, my dad passed away when I was just twenty-five years old, which was a huge loss, and a shock for me and my family. He had sparked my initial interest in wildlife, and especially birds of prey - he was very much a mentor throughout my life. Still, to this day, I miss him terribly.

I often wonder what Dad would think about the fact that now the common buzzard is widespread throughout the UK, and even the red kites are becoming a very common sight across Essex. He probably would not bother reversing up hard-shoulders any more, but I do think he would be just as excited as I am to get a perfect view of these wild creatures.

PART 1

Chapter 1

INTRODUCTION TO FALCONRY

How extraordinary to gain the trust of a raptor.

Even some of the smallest species I have shared my life with exuded power and grace. You cannot make these birds do anything they do not want to; if the bird a falconer casts free isn't happy, it will not return.

Taming and gaining the trust of a raptor takes a lot of time. They are instinct-based flying and hunting machines, which pick from two possible outcomes when faced with strange situations: flight or fight. If you love them, let them go - if it is real, they will come back; even though I don't believe the birds have the capacity for love, I do believe they can most certainly represent it.

Falconry requires absolute trust between handler and bird, and the total freedom to express our wilder instincts - that is what makes falconry so incredible. That, and the amazing ability all birds have, to take to the air and experience a whole new realm, which we humans cannot access.

Before doing falconry professionally, when I kept birds of prey as a personal hobby, I sometimes met members of the public, when I was flying my bird; they would approach me and ask questions about the bird I was flying, which I never minded at all - whatever question they asked, I would answer in full, and always politely. However, whilst I didn't mind answering questions by the public, some of whom had never come across falconry before, it did come as quite a shock to me just how wrongly falconry is perceived, on a mass level.

When I opened my falconry centre to the public, it became even more obvious to me how alien the sport is to people nowadays, especially in urban areas.

After several years of running a falconry centre, I have had various questions raised with me, on a regular basis. Therefore, I decided that by collating the message of what a falconer is, and about the relationship we have with our birds, the message of falconry can finally be available, and helpful to the public.

And, that is the one hope I have for this book: to educate people about falconry. I do not want to go into massive detail about where falconry originated from, or how to train your first bird of prey – there are a thousand books already showing the technical side of falconry.

If you would like to learn falconry on a practical level, I would recommend, after reading this book, to get out there and enrol yourself on to a competent course - use the reading material as a backup to the practical knowledge, which you will gain from such a course.

This book is about why, as falconers, we do what we do, and what we hope to achieve from the methods of training we employ. I also want to show the relationships between myself and my birds of prey. Yes, the human trainer will teach the bird of prey a lot, but, in return, the bird of prey will teach the human more.

We set each other free.

*

So, what is falconry?

It is one of the most intense and successful bonds a human being can have with another living creature; a symbiosis between two separate species, which involves trust, reward, training and dedication.

Over the many thousands of years of civilization, humankind has tamed, trained and domesticated all manner of different animal species; some become beasts of burden, which carry large loads for their owners, while others are employed to guard, love and amuse; some work alongside their humans as heroes, and forge a lasting companionship within their families.

Quite simply falconry is the training of a bird of prey, so that it will return to the falconer's gloved hand, once released to fly and/or hunt. Modern falconry tends to use a variety of birds to catch quarry or prey - falcons, hawks, buzzards and eagles are used as hunting birds.

In the UK, there is a strict season (between 12th August and 1st February) in which specific quarry can be caught with birds of prey, to ensure that no young wildlife is taken, and that the different species permitted to be taken are able to raise their young in good time, in order that they may grow fit enough to outwit, outrun or outfly a raptor, if need be.

Falconry is one of the world's oldest sports – recent information has shown that it could have started in the middle-east, although the earliest known historical documents on falconry are from China, and are dated from before 680BC; the precise origin of falconry will always be difficult to nail down.

Depictions of goshawks and eagles, in early eastern art and poetry, are further indications of just how important and integral falconry was in those cultures at that time.[1]

People in Mongolia still hunt with golden eagles, to this day, and certainly did around the time of 1000BC; their ancestors were using eagles and other raptors for exactly the same reason: primarily, as a practical way to catch food for their families.

One of the earliest documents of falconry was a literary work called "Shinshuu Youkyou", which was commissioned by Emperor Saga in Japan around 818AD.

A more recent document - the Bayeux Tapestry - shows King Harold (England) with a hawk in one scene.

Human beings and birds have worked together for thousands of years. Why? Very simply: we make life better for each other.

A bird of prey soon learns that their human guardian has food. Their entire being is designed to eat and procreate - having a human around, to give them food, makes life easier for them. For the humans, having a winged hunter to assist when trying to catch live prey certainly puts them at an advantage.

*

A person which hunted with falcons would historically be called a "falconer", and a person which hunted with hawks, eagles and buzzards an "austringer". For ease, in this book I will refer to everyone as falconers (we will take it as read that they do, in fact, hunt with falcons) This is also the most commonly used term for people who hunt with birds of prey.

Birds of prey are also referred to as raptors, and I will use this terminology throughout the book.

Chapter 2

RAISING A RAPTOR

The decision to buy a bird of prey takes careful consideration. Once made the human-being agrees to create a partnership with the bird of prey. A lot of time and thought must go into how the bird will be trained and raised, and adequate housing must be provided for the bird. How a bird is housed and kept will vary for each species of bird, as will how the falconer intends to fly the bird; it is, therefore, essential for the falconer to decide which type of bird will suit their lifestyle and needs.

There are different names for a bird of prey, at different stages of its life, and reflecting how it is raised in captivity:

• A young bird of prey is called an "eyass".

• A juvenile raptor, in the first year of its life, is called a "passager".

• An older bird of prey, which has matured beyond its first year, is called a "haggard".

There are three main methods of raising young raptors: "imprinting", "creche-reared" and "parent-reared":

15

Imprinting

A hand-reared bird of prey, which has been raised by human beings, from an early age, is called an "imprint".

Usually, if an imprint is required/preferred, the falconer will let the breeder know this, so that the young bird can be collected when it is around four to six weeks of age - at this stage the bird is a helpless, tiny, fluffy bundle of feathers.

To correctly imprint a raptor requires regular feeding times, throughout the day, and proper training, from early on, to avoid aggression. An imprinted bird of prey will identify as a human-being – it will "imprint" onto its "parent", and see itself as the same kind of species; in the case of a human raising a chick, the chick will think it is human.

An imprint tends to be very vocal, because it will see human-beings as food providers, and providers of parental safety. Imprints are harder to lose in the field, because they are continually looking for you, however, there is a danger that an imprint will be flown at a higher weight in order to stop the bird being so vocal (they call out more when they are hungry) so some imprint birds can wander due to poor weight management which I will explain in later chapters.

With certain species of birds, aggression can show in later years; therefore, it is important to look at the nature of a particular species, before deciding whether or not it is suitable to be hand-reared. Barn owls, for example, are heavily imprinted in this country; they are lovely for the first year, but when they reach sexual maturity, at around eighteen months old, they become nasty around their aviaries - nature tells the barn owl that it needs to kick out at its parents, and either take over the territory, or find its own; that natural instinct still applies, so, as the birds parent, you will see some very stroppy behaviour during the breeding season.

I have three imprint Harris hawks, all of which have different personalities - one even tries to undo my shoelaces, at regular times throughout the day so it's interesting to note that the same imprinting process can have different outcomes depending on the nature of the individual bird.

You are a part of that bird's life, and will have a bond like no other. Imprinting must be done correctly, and implemented on the right species of birds, for everyone to get the best out of life.

Creche-reared

Crèche-reared birds are reared in groups, with other young birds of the same species, or of a species of similar age and size. They will have some human contact, as it will be a person feeding them, instead of a parent bird. They are tamer than a parent-reared bird of prey, as they have had these close encounters with human-kind, but they still know they are birds, having been raised alongside other raptors. They should, therefore, be quieter when resting, and will breed naturally. Creche-reared birds can be easier than full imprints to get hunting.

A lot of people call this method of raising raptors "social imprinting" - it is a very desirable method of rearing nowadays, because you seem to get the benefits of an imprinted bird, without a lot of the noise!

Parent-reared

This is a bird which has been raised by its own kind and has no idea what a human-being is, other than that it is a threat.

A falconer will usually pick up a parent-reared bird at between four and six months old; the birds, by this time, will be "hard-penned" (in full feather), so all of the baby fluff has gone, and the bird will pretty much be ready for training right away. The bird will be almost at full size, so the falconry equipment can be fitted, and the bird can be settled into its new home - with a hefty training process ahead of it.

Parent-reared birds are very calm and quiet, once trained, and will breed naturally, so they can be handy if a particular species is in high demand, or can be used for conservation incentives in the wild.

But, the training process for the falconer is longer, harder and more stressful with parent-reared birds, because they can be quite aloof and independent - it is usually the parent-reared bird which sits up a tree for hours on end, completely ignorant to its falconer, who will probably have lost her voice for calling (yes, I have been that person)!

Still, parent-reared birds make superb hunters and, as they get older, parent-reared birds have such a beautiful nature and a more confident personality in the field. The training process is longer in the beginning however, a trained parent reared bird will be much easier to handle in the later years.

When sexual maturity kicks in, imprints can be a very real problem; they can try to mate with their handlers and become aggressive around food and their territories during the breeding season. A parent reared bird will do no such thing and as the years pass and your bond with the bird grows, they can be just as responsive to the glove as an imprinted bird.

Chapter 3

THE RIGHT BIRD FOR YOU

What is the right bird for you? Well, this depends on your circumstances and what you want the bird to do.

If you are lucky enough to have a lot of flying land at your disposal, but do not want the bird to hunt, then a common buzzard or an owl may well be perfect for you - both of these birds are notoriously lazy.

Once imprinted, they will see you as a parent; they are very happy to fly for you, and to follow you around, but usually without the slightest thought of hunting for themselves - you are their food provider, and they are therefore happy to keep you in their sights, and choose you as their food source, for the rest of their lives.

If you would like a bird to hunt with you should choose a hawk - Harris hawks, sparrow-hawks and goshawks are all good hunters. In fact, goshawks are so well known as good hunters, they were literally called the "cook's bird" in ancient times, because of their ability to fill up the handler's larder with game meat. If you only want to hunt squirrels, rabbits and hare, you could fly a red-tailed buzzard. All of these birds will catch a wide variety of prey, and are very desirable in the falconry community.

Another bird used to hunt hares, foxes and

small deer is the eagle - they are much larger birds of prey and are supreme hunters. Although eagles are not very suitable in some areas of southern England - because they can be very dangerous to small dogs, and because the area does not have the topography eagles really need, to gain lift and soar - they are often used in Scotland, Wales and northern England to hunt quarry in these more remote areas.

Eagles fly best when they have the kind of land which allows them to soar, with clear views of the ground – it is then that they come into their own and hunt as they were meant to, with as few distractions as possible (such as people). This wide space also gives the eagle plenty of thermal currents to ride, without which it can be a very clumsy creature.

Then, there are falcons. Falcons generally differ from eagles and hawks, in that they are much smaller, and faster flyers. They are unique sky hunters, and they can and will cover miles, at extraordinary speeds. Falcons are specialist hunters, which will take birds in mid-air, as well as a huge variety of game on the ground, including rabbits, hares, ducks, moor-hens and even gulls.

Nowadays, it is very common for falconers to have hybrid falcons, which are usually an artificial pairing of two different species, to create a cross-breed. The reason hybrids have become so popular is that they can demonstrate positive attributes from each of the parent species. However, there is a risk with cross-breeding that the bird will have inherited a serious genetic health issue, and/or a bad personality trait, from its parent species. Also, as with most cross-bred species, hybrid falcons tend to be less fertile than their pure counterparts.

I have four falcons at Coda Falconry, two of which are hunting birds; the other two are "demonstration" birds, which like to chase the lure - they do not pay much attention to living quarry.

A good telemetry system is essential with such birds, because if you lose sight of them, they can literally travel miles in a day, if they are chasing something very interesting.

One of my falcons is a saker falcon, which likes to ride thermals to a height of approximately eight-hundred feet, before diving onto her selected target; it can be quite frightening when she goes out of sight, so having the telemetry on her means that I can track her, even if she does decide to catch something miles away.

My other hunting falcon is a peregrine/gyr hybrid. He has a particular fondness for hunting corvids (crows), and I am not over the moon about that, as I also have a raven, which I love dearly; it conflicts with my emotions every time I am left with a dead crow at my feet.

Still, these are predatory animals and, as a falconer, it is my responsibility to ensure that they have a life which equals or exceeds the life they would have had in the wild - hunting and dealing with dead things is part and parcel of being a falconer.

Chapter 4

CAPTIVITY AND CONSERVATION

Falconry can represent a deeper connection between humans and birds, and allow the former to be more in touch with the natural world.

However, the relationship between humans and nature is not always harmonious - as humans compete with each other and nature for space and resources, sadly, it is wildlife which loses out; this includes birds of prey. Habitat loss, hunting and persecution can make the wild a very desolate place for birds of prey, and various species of raptor are now, sadly, in decline in the wild.

Take the saker falcon, for example, which has now been up-listed to endangered species status, due to a very rapid decline in its numbers.[2]

This is the result of our use of agrochemicals, habitat degradation and an unsustainable capture of the bird, for use in falconry. The problem is especially severe in central Asia. To stop the species from going extinct, restrictions must be placed on bird-trapping and egg-collecting; one way to help the saker falcon species survive is by captive breeding, instead of that which happens presently: unregulated capture of the bird, for use in falconry.

However, captive breeding will not assist a

species if the habitat is not there - without the necessary environment, a released raptor cannot hide, when necessary, from other predators, or have enough food to sustain it and its potential brood, should it find a mate.
In addition to habitat destruction is the use of agrochemicals: chemicals used in agriculture - such as pesticides – which can poison the food the birds will eat.

The peregrine falcon was almost wiped out from use of the pesticide DDT (or dichlorodiphenyltrichloroethane); the poisons made their egg-shells so thin that the chick could not survive the incubation period - the outer shells would simply fall apart underneath the parent, while she was incubating them.[3]

Another bird, the hen harrier, is also on the edge of extinction, in this case due to illegal hunting and shooting.

Birds of prey - and other animals – are being saved from extinction by breeding them for captivity; this is where they are not released afterwards, and stay tamed their whole lives. In addition, there are some captive breeding and release programs, which do not rely on habitat for success, and so environment loss is not an issue.

The San Diego Zoo has been able to increase the Californian condor population from twenty-three to two-hundred, through many years of raising captive bred chicks and releasing them, as part of the "Save Wildlife" programme. Zoos, farms and bird of prey centres often feel a duty to educate the public about the animals in their care, in addition to looking after them. Some will set up conservation programs and may even gain funding for local and overseas projects, which will help to safeguard the wild populations. This type of work usually happens quietly, in the background, and the public may not be aware of it.

I have recently taken on many conservation roles in the local area around my falconry centre.

For example, I help out with bird-ringing, so that we can monitor songbird populations and actually track their migration over Europe, to see where they go and how many make it back to us.

Part of my work is also to rehabilitate wild birds of prey, which are brought in to us injured, poorly, starving or a mix of all of these - the main things that we are able to provide injured birds is medication, nutrients and rest.

A wild buzzard was brought into the centre last summer, and was barely recognizable - the bird was tiny, with a broken wing, and his feathers were in tatters; even worse, the injury was infested with maggots. Because the bird had been unable to fly, he had nearly starved to death. An operation was carried out on his wing and he was transferred to a wildlife rehabilitation hospital, pending his release; he was lucky, and survived - most other injured birds would die.

Nature is fragile, hostile and beautiful.

Another example of our conservation work was when we had a Canada gosling handed in to Coda Falconry, early one spring who we decided to call Maverick.

He had been run over on a landfill site, his poor little pelvis had been broken and his bones had re-set in an awkward position - it was impossible to straighten his pelvis. We installed a special paddling pool, just for him, so he could swim and receive some hydrotherapy, which meant his legs grew stronger and he was able to recover.

Soon, he was able to fly, and became somewhat of a nuisance as he decided to take his flight lessons during the middle of our public flying demonstrations which meant that a giant clumsy goose would very often crash land into the arena while we were flying our birds of prey. It was a little confusing for our birds, highly amusing for the audience and absolutely exhausting for our team because sometimes our dear Maverick would need picking up from various points across the farm as he'd tired himself out and couldn't get back to his pool.

He eventually took to the skies to join a migrating flock of geese, which were feeding in the fields behind the centre.

That was a couple of years ago, and I am pleased to say that he has been spotted in the Waltham Abbey gardens on numerous occasions, so we think that is where he has made his home.

As said before, when a bird of prey is flown free, the sky is open to it, and it has no reason to return to the falconer, unless it is happy to do so - that is the free will given to a trained raptor.

It is important to try to give a captive animal the same freedoms which it would have in the wild, but it is also important to realize that captive animals are different to wild animals.

In the case of captive birds, they are humanized - captive bred animals, which have been raised around and trained by humans, with whom they have a very tight bond.

Although the birds can be taught how to develop the instinct, or do so anyway, there are a few species - namely the owls - which cannot catch their own food; they rely on their human guardian to feed them, and would die if released into the wild.

In captivity, a good falconer will strive to allow his bird the right to act out their normal instincts throughout the day - this means making sure the bird is flown free and given everything that it naturally seeks out, including safe shelter and the ability to bathe, during periods of inactivity.

All good zoos, farms and bird of prey centres will automatically be a point of rehabilitation, for injured wild species, at some time or another.

By learning about how our captive animals behave, we can transfer that knowledge to our treatment of wild species - the correct food, medication and housing can be provided, as we have most of what they need, already.

Generally, if the animal's welfare is paramount, then any animal should have a better life in captivity than in the wild - nature is one tough lady, and the animal may be in a constant struggle to survive.

Chapter 5

BIRDS OF PREY IN THE WILD

Wild raptors have my utmost respect and admiration - I still treasure each and every sighting I get of them, especially because they are usually fleeting glances.

I often wonder what errand they are running at that moment - the bird in the air is always very hard at work, and facing a world of hardships, including: looking for food, territory or a mate, or being driven away from an area by competition.

Even though birds of prey are exceptionally good at hunting, and very successful members of the food chain, hunting is still not easy for them - for example: when I take my hawks out hunting, every small bird within a one-mile radius sounds an alarm call, and my bird is mobbed by corvids and other smaller birds, making it very difficult for it to catch anything. Research has shown that healthy, wild raptors successfully catch prey only once in every seven attempts.

One of the hardest things to get through to people that object to falconry on the basis that they "should be free" is the reality of a wild bird's life.

Wild birds don't recognise that they're "free" they only understand that they are hungry or they are not hungry. They have territory or they are fighting for one. They are healthy and they can fly or they can't. Very basic rules but they are the ones that wild raptors adhere to.

If the bird is not 100% fit, it will be unable to survive. Having a meat or protein diet does not enable a bird of prey to store much energy within its body, so resting after a successful kill is essential for energy conservation - no carbs: no energy.

For small, seed-eating birds, with their high metabolism, resting time is short, as they must consume at least 5% of their body weight each day, so they must get back to eating quickly, and consume a certain amount of high energy food, throughout the day. For the most part, raptors do not need to eat as often as the smaller birds - one good meal may be enough for an entire day, or even longer.

On average, a bird of prey will fly for around twenty minutes per day; whether that is searching for food, migrating or finding a territory, raptors use flight only when totally necessary.

Some raptors - namely vultures and eagles - have specialized wings, to help them soar on the thermals, for longer periods of time, in search for food.

But, the same principle applies: they will not be airborne unless required - just the mechanics of flight use up the most energy of any form of their movement, and it is highly inefficient, particularly when paired with a protein diet; every ounce of their being is designed to conserve energy, until the time they need to exert themselves with catching food. They, like most other bird species, also have a very high metabolism, and burning energy without the need to do so is a big problem for them.

In the summer months, when a pair of raptors have young to feed, you will see a lot more birds of prey on the wing - they have a lot of mouths to feed, and a growing family will be a constant strain on the parent birds, which will hunt almost around the clock, to ensure that their brood eats enough to survive.

That said, the mortality rate in some young birds of prey - for example: the peregrine falcon - is about 60%; this means that approximately six out of every ten birds of prey hatched will die in their first year of life. It's a tough life, in the wild.

Every bird of prey which has made it to adulthood has an important role to play within the ecosystem, and it is essential to maintain a healthy environment, so that these predators have a future. Their lives are fleeting and tough, so they deserve our help in making that life a little easier.

I am often asked how we can help make life better for such birds - the answer is simple: love the natural environment and take care of the places that wild birds of prey call home.

Encourage prey into your gardens, by leaving areas of wild grass and flowers, to provide a food source for creatures which could well go on and feed our native raptors; put up nest boxes, and try to entice a nice couple in, that they can raise young and help repopulate their species; pick up litter and take pride in your communal areas - by making the natural habitats more inviting, you will not only help attract more nature into the area, you will make the whole space available to people in the local community.

Taking pride in wild areas is very underrated, yet a shared wild space can be teeming with biodiversity, if given the chance. I believe we should strive to preserve them, to the best of our knowledge and ability.

Chapter 6

COMMON MISCONCEPTIONS ABOUT FALCONRY

I run a falconry centre so often speak to the public and hear their comments on falconry.

Most are lovely observations of the birds, and excitement at seeing them fly on our demonstrations. Some however, are not so favourable, and these comments can be very upsetting for me - and, indeed, anyone who has devoted their life to something, only to have the moral called into question.

Some people believe that birds of prey are not happy unless constantly soaring in the air. But, this is an example of humans projecting our emotions and dreams onto them.

It's ironic that humans in privileged countries "escape to nature" in order to feel free and get some peace, quiet and perspective on their hectic lives. Beautiful log cabins in remote locations offer the best in rose tinted wilderness. It's so easy to be romanced by the beauty of a sunrise and sunset but what is more difficult to comprehend is just how much of a struggle it is for wildlife to survive between those moments. It is literally a constant battle between life and death.

When I'm out flying my birds, I am careful and responsible to notice if there are people ahead. If so I call my bird to the glove and wait for the people to pass. Nine times out of ten, passers-by are in awe of my birds and come over to have a chat. I love moments like that because they are presented with the reality of falconry in that moment.

It's a bond between a human and a bird that can be seen and believed. There's no need to explain that the bird is flown free regularly and will return to me because it wants to, or that it has an easier life than in the wild because I am able to demonstrate exactly that.

My birds are able to experience one thing that their wild counterparts will never be able to know - flying for fun. Nature won't allow the wild birds of prey that frivolous privilege, it would waste far too much energy. They are locked into their survival mode.

Any wild animal is doing what it must to survive, and birds of prey are no exception. Like any predator, they spend most of their lives resting and conserving the energy that they will need to power their flight muscles, to catch their next meal; the life of a wild bird of prey is therefore: eat, sleep, preen, repeat...

Some members of the falconry community have not helped negative public perception, either.

Falconry has, for the most part, been a very elitist hobby, and is still, sadly, made up of some incredibly obstructive people, even in this day and age. That can make it difficult for a huge section of society to gain access to this wonderful sport.

Diversity is something which makes the old school shudder, and I have, on many occasions, been accused by falconers of "bringing the reputation of falconry into disrepute, by teaching it to the underprivileged" - yep, someone really did say that to me!

Due to this cultural barricade, falconry is not practised anywhere near enough in this country, for the general public to have come into contact with it, especially in urban environments. When a person stumbles upon an animal in captivity, which they have not before seen or were not expecting, it can shock them.

As my centre is based on a farm, it is usual that members of the public visiting there are not expecting birds of prey. Upon walking into the bird of prey centre, people become amazed by what they see, and instantly start to question what is in front of them, because it is out of their comfort zone.

I believe that part of this confusion over birds of prey (or, indeed, any perceived "wild animal") in captivity comes from a growing detachment between human-beings and the natural world.

Birds of prey have an almost mystical aura about them; owls have been depicted in Greek mythology, by the owl of Athena, Horus was the falcon god of the ancient Egyptians, and eagles are often used as a symbol of strength and freedom, in many cultures. In our society, we still look upon birds of prey as spiritual beings, which are the true masters of a realm we can never have or own: the sky.

What is freedom?

By definition: The power or right to act, speak, or think as one wants, the quality of being independent of fate or necessity and of not being imprisoned or enslaved.

When a bird of prey is flown free, the sky is open to them and they have no reason to return unless they are happy to do so. They choose their human companion or they do not. That is the free will given to a trained raptor. It is impossible for such a creature to be imprisoned because by definition, they have a choice and if they choose a loving guardian, safe shelter and companionship then so be it. I would too!

So what is it to be wild? Being wild is living or growing in the natural environment without being domesticated or cultivated, without the aid of humans.

Now you can probably see just how different "free" and "wild" really are. Again, with the correct practices of falconry, the trained bird of prey will indeed be living and growing in a natural environment.

When Blue, my Lanner falcon, was just starting to fly, I would pop him on a fence post and just take a walk. He was an imprint falcon and therefore saw me as his parent so he behaved exactly as a branching bird would out in the wild - he followed me when I called him. In doing so, he met the wind and turbulence up in the air and had to learn how to adjust to the shifting environment.

Fresh, daily food is something that no wild raptor has access to and the benefit to the trained bird is very easy to see.

Captive birds of prey are usually larger than their wild counterparts and their feather condition is strong and well-formed due to a good, regular diet. A captive bird won't be teeming with a host of parasites that cause it discomfort on a daily basis and the benefits of a VIP lifestyle is reflected in their life expectancy; birds of prey live on average twice as long as their wild cousins.

Therefore a trained bird of prey is not "imprisoned" at all (as some people think) and can act out their entire life following these principles:

1. Freedom from hunger and thirst.
2. Freedom from discomfort.
3. Freedom from pain, injury and disease
4. Freedom to express normal behaviour
5. Freedom from fear and distress

That's an awful lot of freedom.

Chapter 7

TETHERING AND EQUIPMENT

People often ask me why falconers tether their birds of prey. The reason is that if we let them off together, they would injure and/or eat each other.

The perch on which a tethered bird sits should normally replicate its favoured environment to perch in the wild; falcons mainly sit on flat, rocky surfaces, so they are usually tethered to a block perch, whereas hawks and buzzards prefer to rest on branches, so they will usually be tethered to a bow perch.

A bath should be provided for all tethered birds, so that they can preen, bathe and have a drink, prior to and after their flight.

Tethered birds should be flown free five out of seven days, according to zoo licence standards.

The legs of raptors are extremely strong, and built for endurance - they are not delicate, and even the smallest species of bird can take a huge amount of force and pressure.

A pair of anklets is the kindest and most comfortable way to secure a bird of prey, when it is resting - their legs are tough enough to take any strain caused by "bating" and, as anklets are fitted to the bird throughout its life, they have no impact on any element of its flying activities.

Bating is the term used when a bird of prey

attempts to fly away from its perch, but is still attached. A lot of people think this is a sign of distress and get very upset when they see a bating bird. Yes, in some circumstances it can mean that the bird is upset or frightened by something and its natural instinct is to fly away; however, birds do also bate to stretch their wings, or when they see something very tasty, which they would like to demolish and eat.

Usually, in a falconry centre environment, they will bate towards their falconer, because they know we are the ones who dish out the food.

Because a bird of prey's legs are extremely strong and the process of bating does not hurt the bird at all (as long as they are not bating excessively which no trained bird of prey should do) - they will usually settle down quickly, turn around and jump straight back up on their perch again.

Anklets

Let's start with the first piece of equipment a falconer will put on a bird: the anklets. These are usually made of soft leather, however, there are some very fetching pairs of braided anklets coming onto the market, which are made of a soft nylon material, which is strong and durable – so, you may see brightly coloured booties on captive birds in the future.

At Coda Falconry, I still make and use leather anklets. There are many different styles, but all have the same purpose: to be the anchor for the jesses (the small straps which go into the eyelets formed on the anklets).

Each anklet needs to be modified for the bird it is being fitted to, and is the bird equivalent of shoes – even the same species can have different sized legs, and will therefore require different sized anklets. For this reason, more experienced falconers tend to make their own equipment, as opposed to buying a generic sized anklet from a supplier; it works out cheaper, in the long run, to buy a large leather hide and make perfectly fitting equipment, bespoke for your birds.

They are not shackles, and they are in no way hurting the bird, or chaining it to a spot where it does not want to be - they are simply pieces of leather, through which the jesses slip, via a metal eyelet, which is crafted into the main body of the anklet.

The birds do not even know that they are wearing anklets a lot of the time, and will only actively pick at them if they are new, or if you have a particularly playful bird!

The soft leather absorbs any shock from sudden movements and, like a collar left on a dog, the bird is perfectly happy to wear a pair of anklets its entire life.

Anklets should be changed once a year, to avoid their becoming brittle and breaking. Ideally, they should also be waxed regularly, so that the leather remains supple and comfortable for the bird.

Mews jesses

A jess is a strap which goes through the eyelet on the anklet. They come in a variety of braided nylon versions, and you can, if you wish, put bright pink jesses on your birds. Traditionally these are also made from leather.

They are fed through the eyelets on the anklets, in order to tether a bird of prey; they feature a slit at the end, so that they can be folded over the swivel.

The bird of prey needs a pair of jesses so that the falconer can control when the bird can fly free; using the dog analogy again, it is the same as if you are walking by the side of a busy road - you (should!) have your dog on a lead, until it is safe to let the dog run free. The jesses allow the falconer to tether their birds safely, throughout the day, until it is safe for them to take to the air.

Some birds will bathe in the early morning and not dry out until mid-afternoon, so they cannot fly until their feathers are dry and preened again. Others take a while to cast (bring up their pellet from the day before) and, again, they cannot fly until this has occurred, otherwise it can cause digestive problems.

When the bird is ready, and when the conditions are safe, the falconer can then remove the jesses and swivel from the bird, allowing it to fly free.

Flying straps / flying jesses

These are identical to the mews jesses we put on tethered birds, with only one major difference: they have no slits at the bottom.

The reason this flat piece of leather has no slits at the end is that when flying a bird out in the field, a branch could snag through the slits, as with normal jesses - this could be disastrous for the bird.

Mews jesses have been - and will continue to be - responsible for causing birds to get caught in branches; if they are hanging upside down they may die, if not retrieved quickly enough.

Flying jesses can either be placed on the anklets permanently, or removed each time the bird is flown - the type depends entirely on the preferences of the falconer.

I tend to use permanent flying straps on my birds, because I find it easier, when we are doing quick changes on flying demonstrations, to have the bird ready to go, following the removal of the mews jesses.

Swivel

The swivel is a small piece of metal which can rotate, and is usually made of two parts.

The top part of a swivel is a rough "D" shape, which the jesses can be folded over, in order to hold them in place, when tethering a bird.

The second piece of the swivel is a rotating loop, through which the leash is threaded; due to the fact that this part of the swivel can rotate, it minimizes the risk of the leash becoming tangled. It is an amazing piece of equipment - low tech, but so effective!

It is designed purely to aid the tricky job of securing two jesses with only one hand. As the jesses can be threaded through the middle of the "D" loop and then folded back on themselves, it means the falconer can easily secure a bird of prey, after its flight, with one hand, and then the leash can be put through the rotating loop, at the bottom of the swivel, to further secure the bird. The leash is then usually tied onto the glove, so the bird is safely attached to the falconer.

Leash

The leash for birds of prey is similar to leashes for other animals - they are long leads, used to control the bird in a safe area, until it is ready to fly.

They are usually made of nylon, as it will not break or stretch, like leather does; it is now the material of choice for leashes in the UK and Europe.

Leashes vary in length and thickness, depending on which species of bird you are trying to tether, though all have the same job to do. They are threaded through the loop of the swivel and tied to whichever perch the bird will be sitting on.

For all falconers, the safety of our birds of prey is paramount, and, by tethering a bird, we are keeping it calm and rested, until it has the opportunity to fly free.

In the same way that you keep a dog on a lead, until it is safe to let it off for a run, as a responsible falconer you have to be sure that the environment in which you are choosing to fly your bird is safe, and that no harm will come to you, your bird or the general public, during its free flight.

Falconer's knot

Usually, one of the first things that you will learn as a falconer is the "falconer's knot" - a knot which can be tied and untied with one hand.

This quick release knot features a safety catch, to ensure that the bird of prey cannot undo it, and escape with its full equipment still attached.

Pouch

Most falconers will have a flying jacket or pouch, where the food is stored during a bird of prey's flight.

Telemetry tracker

This comprises a transmitter and receiver.

The transmitter is secured to the bird, prior to its free flight - either by a tail mount, or attachment to the anklet - and the receiver is able to pick up the signal from the transmitter; this allows the falconer, to have an idea of the direction and distance the bird has gone, if it flies out of sight.

A good telemetry system is invaluable, and everyone who flies birds of prey freely should always, without fail, attach a tracker to their bird.

By not doing so, you run the risk of losing your bird, which is careless, and unacceptable in today's modern climate. A non-native bird of prey living wild can cause unheard-of damage to the natural ecosystem, and this is totally avoidable.

So, if you see an aerial-type device dangling from a captive bred bird of prey, please don't panic – you are probably looking at a very well cared for bird, which the owner does not want to lose.

Rouse

This is a term to describe the bird lifting all of its feathers up and shaking itself briskly.

Birds usually rouse as part of their preening routine - by shaking their feathers, they allow dust and debris to fall away from their skin; a bird of prey will usually rouse just before flying, as all of its feathers are now adjusted perfectly, primed and ready for take-off.

In order for a bird of prey to rouse, it must be

comfortable; they do not let their guard down for a second, so, to shuffle all of their feathers and take an eye off of their surroundings - for even a brief moment - requires absolute peace for them.

This is why you will almost never see a wild bird of prey rouse - it will be too frightened of you to relax, if it has spotted you watching it. If you are in a hide, the chances of seeing a bird in this wonderful state of calm will increase, but if you do see a wild bird of prey, being a predator, it will usually be on the lookout for food, so not at its most restful!

In captivity, you will often see birds of prey rouse; they are calm, comfortable and in prime condition. Without a care in the world, a captive bird of prey will rouse several times a day, and will keep its feathers in immaculate condition.

Coping

When a bird of prey has an overgrown beak, it needs to be filed into shape, to stop the bird developing complications when eating. This process is called "coping".

If a beak is left too long, for a considerable amount of time, it can break or crack, which can be extremely painful for the bird; a lot of repair work will then be necessary, to stop further pain and the risk of infection. Both the upper and lower mandible of the beak need filing, in captive birds of prey.

It is inexcusable to see birds of prey which cannot close their beaks, due to the falconer not carrying out coping regularly enough.

Overgrown beaks occur in captive birds of prey because, unlike their wild counterparts, captive birds are fed high quality, nutritional food daily, so their bodies are not starved of the essential vitamins and minerals needed for growth. This means their beaks grow rapidly; they are made of keratin (the same material as our hair and fingernails), so, just as when we eat well, our hair and nails grow longer and at a faster rate, so it is with a bird's beak.

The process of coping a beak is very simple and can be likened to having your fingernails filed into shape. It has to be done carefully, though, holding the bird securely to avoid the risk of a nasty nip or grab from the bird, or the risk of damage to its beak.

Cast

Every day, a bird of prey will produce a pellet, which it will regurgitate from its digestive system and spit out of its beak.

Owl pellets are famously shown around schools, or any kind of field-craft event, so a lot of people will be familiar with them; some may have even dissected a few pellets in their time, exposing all the bones which are encapsulated inside, and identifying what the owl has eaten!

What surprises most people is that all birds of prey produce a pellet. All of the indigestible material in their prey (fur, bones and teeth) is formed into a pellet, in the bird of prey's gizzard.

About six to ten hours after eating, the bird of prey will then regurgitate this pellet, which, as it is coming up through the digestive tract, will also clean out the gullet and promote better internal health.

Falconers must therefore give their bird of prey "casting" - any item of food the bird will eat which has fur, feathers or some kind of roughage within it - so that the bird can produce a pellet.

Before we fly our birds of prey, it is essential to look at whether the bird has cast a pellet, because you cannot have new food going in before the old food has come out - this can lead to a whole host of digestive problems, and can contribute to "sour-crop", an infection in the bird of prey's crop, due to the fact that it has not been cleaned out by proper casting.

Gauntlet

This is the leather glove that falconers use, in order to carry their birds around, and call to, during their flight.

Usually the gauntlet is on the falconer's least dominant hand, as they will need their good hand to tie and untie the "falconer's knot". There are, of course, left- and right-handed gauntlets, in this amazing modern age.

Lure

This is normally a leather pad, which is attached to the end of a piece of rope; the rope is wound around its handle, and the falconer can then swing the lure in one hand, whilst holding the rope's slack in the other.

Lures are used to engage falcons in flight, although some now train several species of raptor to the lure, because it can help with retrieval, out in the field.

A swung lure is a very attractive target for a trained bird of prey, because it knows that there is a big reward at the end of it! Food is tied around the leather pad (tightly!) and, when swung, it replicates a bird in flight - for raptors specializing in catching birds (falcons and some hawks), the lure is irresistible.

They will chase this moving target until they are truly worn out, and can be called to the lure, once they have finished their flight; it really is the best way to exercise falcons, and can make for some extremely breath-taking demonstrations!

Creance

A very complicated name for a piece of string!

The name "creance" is dated from the late fifteenth century, and from the French word "créance", which means "faith". In falconry terms, it denotes a cord used to retain a bird which is "peu de créance" ("of little faith"); a bird which cannot yet be relied upon will have the creance fitted. The creance can be removed, once the bird of prey has good recall over a long distance.

It is a long cord, which is usually coated with

oils or wax, to stop it snagging on foliage. Like the lure, it is wound around a handle, so that the falconer can hold the creance and keep it secure, whilst the other end of the cord is tied to the swivel of the bird.

We only use a creance on birds which are in training, as we are trying to get an idea of their flying weight, before we let them fly free.

Chapter 8

PUBLIC OBSERVATIONS

Our falconry team has heard it all, from a man bowling up to me during a static display, and exclaiming: "I carve tits" (of course, he meant the bird variety but it was amusing all the same) to people asking us how owls have sex; there is very little we have not had to explain to our audience, during the many demonstrations we have given around the country.

I thought I would include a list of the questions we are frequently asked and the answers to each, in the hope that people can make sense of what they see at a falconry display in the future:

Are the birds of prey bothered by people?

Thankfully, the answer is no!

The birds taken out on displays are some of our calmer individuals, which are used to being travelled, and are perfectly happy to fly in strange environments. All of our birds are born and raised in captivity, so they are humanized, and perfectly happy and comfortable around people.

We select the best birds for the environment; for example, there is no use in taking a falcon to an area with pylons or overhead cables, as they could incur serious injury if they were to collide with them.

We do our homework, and for any new contract which is asking for a flying demonstration, we ask for photos of the flying arena area, so that we can judge whether or not it is actually possible, and if so, which birds would perform best there.

Any falconry display should have a sheltered area and a barrier around the birds, to stop people getting too close, while they are resting on their perches. As long as the falconer in charge is sensible and respectful of the birds' needs, they will be quite content to sit on their perches for the duration of the display. Remember: the birds you see may not be tethered all the time back at their home, but it is essential to tether them on a display, as they are in close proximity to each other.

How do you travel the birds?

Each individual bird of prey has its very own transportation box - these are specially made to house birds of prey.

Good falconry centres should have a transportation licence, which lists all of the birds which will be travelled, and limits the amount of time that a bird can legally be in its box (Coda Falconry's licence stipulates a maximum of eight hours).

The travel boxes come in a variety of different sizes, to accommodate any species of raptor you may need. They are well ventilated, dark boxes, with a perch running through the middle of them, so the birds can safely grip onto something during the drive, and are not stressed by being able to see outside of the box.

What do the birds eat?

Most things which are considered cute and furry, like rabbits, day-old chicks, hamsters, guinea pigs, mice and rats. They also eat a lot of game meat - for example: pheasants, ducks, moorhens, geese and quail.

All of this food must be fed raw and, a lot of the time, we have to prepare the food before we give it to our birds. Game animals and rats tend to be disembowelled, to remove most of the toxins from the meat (believe me, this really does make you smell bad for the entire day; falconry is definitely not a glamorous career choice!).

Do birds of prey make good pets?

No, absolutely not! If I had a pound for every time I was asked this, I would be very rich.

The reality is that trained birds of prey and knowledgeable falconers make it look far too easy - someone with absolutely no clue about falconry, or the gruelling training period it requires, may look at someone flying a bird free and think: Wow! I can do that!

It takes a lot of time, money in the initial stage, effort and patience to look after a bird of prey. The skills required to raise and train a bird of prey can take months - even years - to master properly.

Also, depending on the species, a bird of prey can live a long time; on average, a Harris hawk can live up to twenty years in captivity. The prospective falconer will need to be that bird's hunting/flying partner for the duration of its life. They will need an area suitable to fly a bird free, or access to nearby land where they can. Also, they should consider how their neighbours are going to feel about a potentially noisy predator in their back garden.

Too many people buy a raptor on a whim, have no clue what to do with it and end up losing the bird, because they did not put the groundwork in on training it, did not put telemetry on it, or they just cannot be bothered to look for it; they would rather go and buy another one (raptors are relatively cheap to buy), instead of considering why they lost their bird in the first place. Then, the whole sorry circle starts again.

Don't get me wrong - losing a bird of prey does happen to the best of us, at some point in our lives; there are a lot of factors involved - like weather, accidents when flying or predation by another species - when out in the field, but these should only happen once in a blue moon.
In most cases, people put the bird up for sale, as they can no longer look after it. When I see the phrase "selling through no fault of its own" on a bird-selling website, my blood boils; no - it certainly was not the bird's fault. Still, the

chances are it is going to exchange hands time and time again, because no-one buying it has any clue how to deal with a now-troubled bird, and it will be utterly ruined.

The amount of Harris hawks now living wild in the UK just shows that something needs to be done to licence birds of prey – it is unforgivable that a creature which requires specialist knowledge and care can be sold so easily, and lost so carelessly.

Birds of prey are not pets - they are working animals, which need constant manning, training and focus, in order to get the best out of them.

If you would like to know more about falconry, and how to train your first bird, please go to one of the many falconry centres around the UK, which run courses on how to look after a bird of prey; then, if you are still serious, volunteer at a centre, to see first-hand how difficult they are to look after properly.

Are you sure birds of prey don't make good pets? Because, my uncle Fred kept a buzzard and an eagle-owl in his back garden for years!

Yes, I'm sure Fred did.

But did he train them and fly them free? If the answer is no, then Fred probably wasn't doing the best thing for those birds. Instead of replicating that, it is important to educate people on the proper care and requirements of raptors, which is why attending a course, and/or volunteering, is so important as a first step towards falconry.

Without falconry being taught on a more visible level, we open ourselves up to people over-breeding popular species, and those birds then being sold to anybody, regardless of their experience.

This is another reason why legitimate falconry centres are so important: not only can we mentor people, with regards to training their own bird, but we can also educate people on the correct practices of housing and flying these beautiful raptors.

Do you need a licence to keep a bird of prey?

Sadly not. In the UK, there is very little legislation, and anyone can legally obtain any species of raptor.

Native birds, which have been bred in captivity, require what is called an "Article 10" certificate, which proves the bird was not taken from the wild - this relates to the bird's closed ring, which was popped on its leg, at around ten- to twelve-days old.

A falconry licence is required by law, for anyone flying a bird of prey free in a public area. However, this only indicates what the bird is allowed to hunt, and not the ownership of the bird itself; it is up to reputable breeders to ensure that the birds they are selling are going to a knowledgeable home - this can help to stop them falling into the wrong hands.

Other than that, most people can purchase birds of prey, either online or through breeders, with no form of licence

Do your birds always come back?

Yes.
I have had to track birds for several days on occasion, because I messed up the weight on a young bird, or something has spooked the bird while it was flying. But, as long as any bird you fly free has telemetry fitted to it, and is at a good weight to be responsive, a trained bird of prey should always find its way back to the glove.

How do you get your birds to come back to you?

The answer is "manning" - that is handling a bird, so that it trusts you are not going to harm it - and weight control.
We either hand-rear our birds from young chicks, so they have a parental bond with us, or we spend long days taming a parent-reared bird, by feeding it on the gloved hand, picking it up, walking around with the bird on the glove, and putting it back down on its perch, so it gets used to being close to a human.
Alongside that, we feel the bird's feet, chest and legs, so it becomes used to the sensation of being touched - this helps when we have to put equipment on the bird, or feel the breastbone ("keel"), to check if it is in "good condition"; a bird

in good condition will have a bit of meat/muscle around the breastbone, while a bird in low condition will have a very sharp keel, with little to no flesh around it.

When the birds are comfortable around people, we begin to jump them to food, and mark their weight daily, to assess when and at which weight they were more responsive – this is the start of finding out what their flying weight is.

What we call the "flying weight" is the ideal, optimum weight for a bird of prey, in order to fly free: if a bird is overweight, it will sit in a tree and look at you as if you are insane, not moving until it is hungry enough to do so; if a bird is underweight, it will not have the energy to fly, and will be extremely lethargic, in the same way that we would be, if we were starving - the flying weight is the happy medium between these two extremes, and will result in a happy, obedient bird of prey, which will return to your gloved hand perfectly.

Once a flying weight is established, we get the birds to fly to food on a gloved hand, over longer and longer distances, until we feel they are ready to fly free.
If you have done your training, manning and weight control well, when you release your bird to fly free, it should return to the falconer after its free flight.

Do you hunt with your birds?

Yes. Most of my flying team - including six

Harris hawks, a peregrine/lanner falcon and a red-tailed buzzard - are trained hunting birds.

Out in the field, they have caught geese, rabbits, moorhens, ducks, rats, a chicken (an unexpected whoopsie-daisy there), a worm, crows, and Poppy, my female Harris hawk, decided she would wrestle with a lump of wood she spotted in the long grass.

It is their job to find and catch food, for them and the other birds at the centre to eat, which not only stimulates their innate desire to hunt, but also helps the bank balance, when it comes to the food bill!

The bird usually grabs its prey by the head and back - once it has bound into the prey's body, tightly, with its talons, it will crush its prey, and stab it with kicking movements. As a falconer, it is your job to dispatch the prey humanely, as the birds are rather cruel in their manners, and will start eating their catch while it is still alive.

Isn't it cruel to hunt other living things?

If you are a predator, then no.

Birds of prey do not know the meaning of right and wrong - they only follow their instincts, which are to hunt prey for them to eat. It is built into their survival mode, whether they were born in the wild or captivity - the desire to catch prey is so ingrained in some species, that they will usually exhibit hunting behaviour as they mature. Some birds need a little extra help, training or encouragement to hunt, but, in the main, a bird of prey is a perfectly-honed killing machine.

As a human guardian, it would be cruel to deny an active hunting species the right to catch its prey, as was intended. A lot of the time, a bird of prey will give chase, and not catch anything, but at least they were given the chance – it is important stimulation and enrichment for the birds.

That said, excessive hunting in one area, or throughout the summer months, is detrimental to the environment (and thoroughly illegal, thankfully). When there are young animals around, it is best to put your hunting birds in moult, so the populations of your prey animals remain steady, and they have quarry to pursue the following season.

Can you make the bird look at my camera?

Sure thing!
Oh, wait - it's a bird, not a robot! I'm afraid you'll just have to wait for it to turn its head.

Why is it an owl?

Erm… Well, it was born an owl…

Are they real?

Yes, they most certainly are.

The Author Sarah-Jane Manarin with Fortune.

The Human Team at Coda Falconry.

A public flying demonstration at Coda Falconry.

Another part of a public flying demonstration at Coda Falconry.

Logan from Coda Falconry.

Dizzy from Coda Falconry.

Otis from Coda Falconry.

Loki from Coda Falconry.

PART 2

When I first started my falconry business, back in 2012, competitors started an online hate campaign against me, ridiculing my knowledge of falconry and my business, with the sole intention of getting me shut down before I became big enough to challenge their set up; the falconry forums were alive with appalling comments which were very distressing to read.

Not only did I have to deal with serious damage to my business just after it opened, I also had to contend with online bullying on social media, various falconers coming to my little set-up to intimidate me, and death threats, via text messages on my phone.

As you can imagine, it was not too pleasant to deal with and, as the pressures and bullying escalated, I started the slow dive of oblivion into depression - I would wander, emotionless, through a sea of days, completely numb to the outside world, and wishing that everything would just go away. It started with tears, and ended in me simply not wanting to exist any more; this, in turn, affected my ability, even, to function.

The only thing that got me out of bed each morning was the fact that I had to look after my birds - they needed to be flown, fed and cared for.

One night, as tears rolled down my face, after being attacked by the online bullies once again, one of my birds, Otis, hopped over to me and nuzzled my hand with his beak bristles, as if to say: "It's okay - they can't harm you in here".

The slightest level of affection, when you are

staring depression in the face, is life changing. If no-one else cared, or wanted me to succeed... well, that was fine, but this little owl was rooting for me. If I did not carry on, he would have nowhere to call home; I used to think that I would do it for him.

So, I decided to carry on with what I was doing, following my dream and making my family proud.

I contacted the police, in relation to the harassment and threats; in the end, thankfully, an injunction was set on the people involved.

The next thing I did was take myself off the falconry forums, withdrawing from the falconry "community", and starting to love myself again.

I carried on flying my birds, giving my customers the best experience-days they could imagine, and growing my customer base, until I had a lot of bookings throughout the year, and was starting to see my centre shaping up for the future.

As the good reviews started to pour in, and the centre began to grow, I could finally put all my fears to rest - I had proved that I could run a good falconry centre, in which the birds' welfare was paramount, and our customers would be treated to exceptional experiences.

Re-bookings are always a good sign of a well-run centre, and we started to get lots of them!

Given the time which was needed to grow the centre, I was able to silence my critics with my success, which, in many ways, is the best way to go about these things.

I read something a little while ago, which said: "When they tried to bury you, they didn't realize you were a seed." I think that is a very apt quote for what I encountered in those early days.

The most important thing I remember is that none of this would have happened, without my birds - they are the reason I fought depression.

Without them, I would not have had the energy, or wanted to carry on; it is no understatement to say that they saved my life. I would now like to share with you stories about some of the birds I have had the pleasure to share my life with.

Chapter 9

FORTUNE

Fortune is a red-tailed buzzard.

These birds have always been a particular favourite of mine – they are an extremely under-rated falconry bird in England. They go by other names, including "red-tailed hawk" and "chicken hawk", even though they are not hawks - they are buzzards, as reflected in their Latin name: buteo jamaicensis (buteo meaning "buzzard"). So, here in the UK we call them red-tailed buzzards.

Fortune is, like a lot of red-tails, stubborn. Like, seriously: "I think I'm going to sit in a dark corner, and let the frustration ease off before I even look at you again" kind of stubborn. It took me two months just to get Fortune to recall. Compare this to my Harris hawk, which only took a little over three weeks to train, right up to catching her first kill.

Fortune is also extremely powerful - his optimum flying/hunting weight is 2lb-1oz. (yes, we do use pounds and ounces when calculating the weight of birds - some traditions don't change); he has a lot of muscle and bulk below those feathers. Female red-tails easily reach flying weights from 2lb-5oz. to 3lb-2oz.

Fortune has the most amazing feathers. If you have never seen a red-tail up close, I recommend you go to a falconry centre to look at one.

In its first year, a red-tail has a chocolate-brown coloured tail, which blends into its main body plumage. My best friend, Kate, once remarked that a juvenile red-tail looked like "vanilla ice cream with milk chocolate ripples running through the middle", and, to this date, I have never found a more accurate way to describe this colour variation.

Lots of birds of prey have a different look, when they are in their first year. Their "first year plumage" is a fascinating evolutionary trait of survival - the distinct look is a signal to other birds of prey in that area: by essentially looking different, their same species can identify them as young birds, and therefore not a threat to the territory.

This important signal allows the young, inexperienced bird to learn how to hunt and survive, without the added hardship of having to deal with some angry adult birds, which will attack without mercy, if they feel that their status within a territory is threatened.

Birds of prey will pair up and work as a "strike force team" against an impostor or foreign bird in their territory, and will screech and dive at it, attempting to knock it out of the sky; even if the foreign bird beats a retreat, it is still likely to be pursued for some time.

Life is most definitely hard for wild birds of prey, and this is nature's way of taking pity on the youngsters, and given them a helping hand in their first year.

Fortune is now nearly five years old, with his full adult plumage. Chocolate and off-white feathers on the body give way to the most beautiful hues of red, ginger and autumnal browns; big, chunky swathes of colour suddenly disperse into generous flecks of delicate cream, grey and black, like a hand-painted masterpiece.

Fortune's tail also lives up to his namesake - his chocolate brown baby-tail is now a rich collection of russet red feathers, which fan out in flight.

Fortune is still relatively young.

Red-tailed buzzards can live up to twenty-seven years in captivity, and only about half of that in the wild.

I still remember meeting him, when he was a baby, in his breeder's garden, way back in the summer of 2012. I had found a temporary base, from where I could start my new falconry business, but there was only one problem: I did not have any of my own birds! After years of working and volunteering at falconry centres all over the country, I had always flown and trained THOSE birds so it never occurred to me to get my own.

So, I started looking for a Harris hawk on breeders' websites when something caught my eye:

"Red-tailed buzzard for sale – Essex; has been flown; one-year old; great temperament."

OOOOOH! I pondered - it certainly wasn't a Harris hawk.

Well, what's the worst that can happen? I thought. Let's phone the breeder.

I dialled the number and a lovely guy answered the phone - he gave me some of the history of the red-tail, and what it was like. Then, he did something which always fills me with confidence: he interrogated me!

Well, it was really vetting me. I wish that more sellers would do this. In a country which does not require any form of licence, the first line of defence for birds of prey in captivity is whether or not the breeder is going to sell them to a knowledgeable home. Knowing that I was talking to a sound breeder gave me the confidence to know that he cared about his birds, and if a breeder cares about his birds, they are going to be well-bred.

So, that was that. I booked a day to come and look at this red-tail, and suddenly felt very excited! My first bird could well be arriving home with me, soon.

It was such a beautiful summer's day, and I found the breeder's house fairly easily (which is a miracle for me!). He introduced me to a stunning red-tail, which was sitting in a very relaxed pose in his garden - standing on one leg, aloft his specially made bow perch.

WOW!

He was a beauty. Still in his juvenile plumage, this red-tail had eyes to die for – they were piercing and intelligent. Not a blemish on his feet, nor a feather out of place; eyes bright, nasal canals clear and general character feisty and confident. Perfect! I fell in love with him there and then, and bought him.

I knew just from seeing him that he was going to be a stubborn little bugger, and when I reached out my gloved hand to check him over, this became even more clear.

Even though the breeder had worked with this bird, it had not had one-to-one training for a long period of time (breeders do not want to pour their efforts into a bird which is inevitably going to be sold), so was what I would call "unmanned" (or, did not understand that humans are, in fact, friends), which is very typically the case when you pick up a parent-reared bird to train. What this means is lots of bating!

So, we had a very flappy few minutes, before I managed to calm the red-tail enough for him to sit on my glove. He was gorgeous. I promised to keep the breeder informed of his progress, and boxed the little man, ready for his trip to his new home.

On the car journey, I suddenly realized that this young bird was the start of things for me - to put previous experiences in the falconry world behind me, and start a centre which would be different; one which would, essentially, welcome and introduce people from a largely urban area to the concept of falconry, provide information about birds of prey in a new way, and be focused on conservation.

A character sprang to mind, about a hero in

a book I had read, which stood for survival, in the face of horrific opposition…

Fortune. His name would be Fortune.

I couldn't wait to get Fortune back, and used to his new home.

When I arrived, I tethered Fortune to a large bow perch in the back garden, placed a large bird of prey bath beside him and filled it with fresh water, all under his quizzical stare. Five minutes later, he was taking full advantage of his new paddling pool, plunging into the water, ruffling and shaking his feathers, until he was absolutely drenched. After perfecting the "soggy" look, he happily hopped up onto his bow perch again, and outstretched his soaking wings into the late afternoon sunshine, to dry off.

I settled him into his new weathering later that night, just after the sun had set, so he could sleep peacefully, ready for tomorrow.
The next day, I went out to look at our new team member, to make sure he had settled in nicely.

He had - Fortune was once again relaxing on one foot, his feathers puffed out, his eyes bright and shiny, taking in the whole world.

Before I popped him out onto the bow perch again, I wanted to change the falconry equipment which was already on him, as I never really trust old leather – by my thinking: if I have made and put the equipment on, myself, I know exactly how old it is, and what it has been through.

My paranoia over this started when I did a static display, at a centre I used to volunteer with; the head falconer tethered a Bengal eagle-owl out in front of the general public, with the worst equipment I had ever seen - the leather was brittle and hard on the bird's leg and, no sooner had the bird been tethered, it bated, and both anklets snapped, allowing the frightened bird to fly off, into a line of trees, at the back of the field where the display was being held.

A totally unnecessary panic ensued, for the falconry team and for members of the public (who saw the whole thing), and it made us all look rather silly. The Bengal eagle-owl was finally retrieved from the trees by the head falconer, about an hour after its escape, which was extremely lucky, as a frightened owl can disappear for days.

This just shows how important the basics of falconry are: mistakes can and will happen; the unthinkable can occur, but as a falconer, it is your job to try to minimize these situations, using prevention rather than cure.

I cut a pair of anklets for Fortune, out of super-strong kangaroo-hide, as I knew that this material could withstand a real beating; while I was in a cutting leather mood, I also fashioned him a pair of jesses. I was not sure how I was going to do this, since Fortune didn't know me too well, and there was the danger that he would lash out with his talons or beak (or both!), and try to get away from me, as soon as I had taken the old leathers off - a two-pound red-tail doing any of this would make this day a particularly bad one.

Aside from the fact that Fortune did not know me that well, he was in a strange environment and extremely fat, which meant that he had no real reason or need for human attention at all.

Changing his anklets would require my cutting off the old ones, putting moisturizer onto his feet to keep the skin supple, and then replacing them with the new soft, leather anklets I had just made – that is a lot of strange behaviour for a bird of prey to cope with, if it has not yet got a bond with you; the inevitable reaction to this whole process is a struggling, biting, footing bird. Indeed, with brand new birds which have come straight from the breeders, it is essential that the bird is cast, or held at the shoulders and legs by another person, to stop bird and falconer getting injured while the equipment is fitted.

Fortune, however, was not exhibiting any kind of aggressive or fearful behaviour towards me, as I picked him up from the weathering. So, instead of stressing him, by grabbing him by the shoulders, I thought I would try my luck, and see if he would sit steady upon my glove, whilst I cut off his old booties - as I raised the snippers to the first old anklet, he did not even flinch. With very careful motions I set about cutting the leather on his left leg, until it dropped off, to reveal the bare skin.

I was amazed at just how chunky Fortune's legs were. All red-tails have very thick legs, with large and powerful feet; the skin around the top of the foot is very wrinkled in texture and large plates of extra skin overlap, right the way down to the ends of the toes and talons. The extra skin is almost like armour plating, which comes in very handy, when considering the food they like to hunt - one of their favourites is the grey squirrel, which happens to have an enormously powerful bite, which can completely sever the tendons, and even bones, of most birds. But, not so with a red-tail - the extra skin and plating on their feet allows them to hunt grey squirrels with relative ease, because if they catch one, and it turns to bite them in defence, the tough skin protects their feet, and the squirrel can do relatively little damage.

With the old leather now removed from his left leg, I was able to put some moisturizing cream onto the entire leg and foot, which would ensure that his skin had less chance of becoming too dry, and cracking.

If this happens, it can increase the chances of a whole host of potential problems, including infections and the disease dreaded by any falconer: "bumblefoot". What may sound like a character in a children's cartoon, is, in fact, a very nasty condition, which affects areas of the feet, on many species of birds, including parrots, chickens and - you guessed it - birds of prey.

When an open wound is left without treatment, bacteria enters the cut and causes horrendous sores, swellings and infection, which can be fatal if not treated.

As with most things: prevention is better than cure.

Moisturizing Fortune's feet - what an interesting way to start the day, I thought, as I squeezed the cream onto a toothbrush.

He sat there, on my glove, beautifully, and showed absolutely no signs of wanting to sink his generous talons into my hand. Still, I did not really want to take the chance; I am always astonished at just how quickly even the largest birds of prey can move, when they want to, and I had no wish to be on the receiving end of any quick reflexes!

By putting the cream onto the end of a toothbrush, I was able to reach the bottom of Fortune's foot, and really get into all the nooks and crannies of his pads. As I massaged the cream into his feet with the toothbrush, he lifted his foot, ever-so-slightly, so that I could get right in there and give him a much-deserved pedicure; he seemed to be thinking: Oooh, yes - this is the life. Carry on, human! So, I happily obliged.

Once his feet were suitably pampered, I finally put on the new anklet - called a "false Aylmeri" - and secured it, by wrapping it around his leg with two folds. When I had finished, Fortune had two new anklets and a brand-new pair of jesses.

Over the next few weeks, I would carry Fortune around with me as much as possible – he would sit on my glove while I was watching TV, I would walk him around the garden and in local fields and, between these important manning sessions, I would attempt to feed him on the glove.

It took a good week, before Fortune felt comfortable enough to take his first meal from the glove. He eyed me nervously the day he made this milestone, peeking at me, then at the food, then back at me for a couple of minutes, before his natural instinct to feed took over the fear he had of humans.

He trusted me now - a bond was forged; I meant him no harm and he knew this, implicitly.

After he had polished off his first day-old chick, he was looking at me with a new emotion: excitement. "Well, that was easy!" he almost chirped.

I popped another chick onto the glove, which was taken with much enthusiasm; his nose was now running, to lubricate the beak, and he had officially clicked into "food mode". After four chicks, his crop was bulging, and he had a very satisfied expression indeed; he actually said thank you, in his own way, by sneezing and covering my face with nasal juice and chick yolk.

Yummy.

*

It was not long before Fortune was flying. Once a bird of prey trusts its handler, the training process speeds up, from getting absolutely nothing out of the bird – other than flapping away from you - to the bird flying free. Fortune weighed 1lb-15oz. - a good weight for a young bird.

I tied Fortune to my glove a few days later,

and got him to jump to my glove for large chunks of food, so he would be well rewarded for coming towards me. He absolutely nailed it!

By the end of the month, Fortune was flying at about twenty-feet, on the creance – he was very responsive to smaller bits of food, and I was getting more flights out of him. Great! I thought; Next time we'll fly him free!

I cast him off, to a fence which surrounded the fields I had walked him around, during the manning process, confident that he was the same weight as yesterday, when he had flown brilliantly. I expected him to do a perfect recall.

I was wrong - I must have forgotten that Fortune was a red-tailed buzzard!

Fortune sat, a little bemused, on the fence, and checked out a rather large, tall tree, which was situated to the right of him; he started bobbing his head. I didn't like the fact that he was bobbing his head in the direction of this tree! It means only one thing: Ooooh, that looks interesting.

This is fine if the head is bobbing in my direction, but not when it is toward a hundred-foot conifer.

Fortune then went and took himself off to the very top of the conifer, where he took on a weather-vane pose, without even a second glance in my direction; I had absolutely no hope of his being interested in food: the world was far more interesting than me, from this new, lofty height.

Every falconer has that one moment (well,

several actually), which makes them look ridiculous - this was mine.

Normally, the private field I was in was empty.

Not today.

A memo must have been sent out to everyone in the area: there will be a lady, frantically flapping a dead chick on a glove, whistling and calling a bird, in varying tones, with no result, whatsoever! Several people approached and began questioning me:

"Will he come back?" I surely hoped he would.

"Is that your bird?" - the answer to which I thought was fairly obvious.

"Is he real?" This one, quite frankly, blew my mind - mainly because I wished he was, in fact, a robot, so that I could remotely control him down and leave, with at least some of my dignity intact.

By the time I had been asked the umpteenth question, and a crowd had started to form, it was time for me to admit defeat. He had telemetry on (I would never fly a bird free without telemetry), so, as it was obvious that he was not interested in food and the light was fading, I decided to call it a night; he needed to be a little hungrier, in order to respond to me.

That night I did not sleep, and was already up when my alarm beeped at four a.m. I shut it off, got dressed and marched myself down to the fields, just as the sun was beginning to rise. I went back to Fortune's conifer, and was not surprised that he was not within view there.

So, I got my telemetry receiver out and picked up a signal - it led me to the largest rapeseed field in bloom that I have ever seen; full of yellow on a colossal scale - a never-ending blanket of gold, with the most pungent smell in the world. It was so overwhelming, I sneezed several times, before thinking: No - he can't be in there!

I turned the telemetry to a near setting, hoping amongst hope that it would lead me away from this overly sweet field of yellow. But, no - it kept pointing to a direction which would, basically, lead me directly into the middle of it!

The farmer is going to love me, was my next observation.

My thoughts were jolted out of action when my mobile phone started ringing – it was Kate. I told her about the missing Fortune incident, and she agreed to come and help get him back; it is so much nicer having company in situations like this, not least of all because when there are two of you, you suddenly don't seem such a plonker!

I told her where I was, and decided to chill, until she got to me.

Not far ahead of me, a skylark flew upward, in a vertical motion, singing his beautiful song into the new late-summer day. I watched the tiny little lark ascend to an incredible height, almost dancing in the air, climbing higher and higher, until he was a tiny speck, in a beautiful, cobalt sky.

To this day, the song of a skylark always

stops me in my tracks; sadly, they are very rare to hear nowadays.

Finally, Kate found me and greeted me with a big hug.

"You're not going to believe this, but the telemetry is saying that Fortune is in the middle of that field," I gestured toward the blanket of pungent yellow.

"Oooooh… okay. You are aware that I have hay-fever, right?" replied Kate.

"Um… Well, technically it's not hay, so you should be fine," was my helpful response.

So, there we stood, facing a five-foot high wall of solid rapeseed crop. I checked the signal on the telemetry again, and pushed through the first few layers. The signal was bouncing around, which was to be expected, but I had a general main direction.

After about fifteen minutes of trekking through the crop, being assaulted by bugs and spiders (which seem to build cities at the bottom of rapeseed crops, let me tell you), tripping over unexpected brambles and being absolutely drenched by rain-water, which had become trapped in the thick leaves, we saw something flapping, about twenty feet in front of us. Kate spotted it first and, through her sneezing and coughing, she pointed to a spot to the right of where we were walking.

"Did you see him?" I called.

"Well, I can't say for sure, but there is definitely something causing a commotion over there; I saw wings!"

Good enough for me. That was where we started walking to.

By now, the telemetry was pinging "10" on the near channel, in all directions - this means that the transmitter (which is, hopefully, still attached to your bird) is literally within your grasp. Fortune had to be within almost tripping distance. I could not see above the crops at this point; we were at least fifty feet into the crop and it was thick – visibility was non-existent and the smell was overwhelming. The only thing I could think would work was to crouch down and look through the stems, to see if I could catch a glimpse of my elusive red-tail.
Nothing, yet.

Then, something cracked in the distance, and made a dull thud, as though it had just hit the floor.

"Can you hear that?" I called to Kate.

She crouched down next to me, and we stayed dead silent.

Sure enough, there came another sound: this time a rustling in the undergrowth, not too far from us. I whistled, as Fortune was used to a whistle call to signal food; then, I started to head, very slowly, towards the noise.

I spotted him.
There was Fortune - drenched, his beak open and a fierce expression on his face (which basically meant that he blamed me entirely for his predicament). Yellow pollen clung to his feathers, making him look like a ferocious canary; all dignity had left him.

Fortune spotted me, as I whistled to him. But, before I could get the food out of my jacket and place it on my gloved hand, he hung his wings down either side of his body, and unceremoniously started walking towards me. He shuffled through the thick stems and came to rest, right in front of me, as I was crouched on the floor.

"You silly arse!" was all I could bring myself to say to him. I offered my glove and he leapt onto it. The food was obviously very welcome, as, within two seconds, he was munching on all that was presented to him - this allowed me to put all of his equipment back on him, and tie his leash to my glove.

We had him! I was elated, Kate was sneezing (though, also elated) and Fortune had learnt a valuable lesson about rapeseed crops. He never went wayward again!

*

In the following years, Fortune became an incredible hunting bird - I have caught many rabbits and grey squirrels with him, season after season.

But, what makes me count my blessings even more, with Fortune, is that he is an exceptional demonstration bird. When the hunting season ends, I bring Fortune out, into our flying arena; he astonishes the crowds at Lee Valley Park Farm every day, by soaring over their heads, swooping from the trees surrounding the park and showing off the many beautiful colours in his plumage, which he has now developed. Fortune has even helped to raise money at charity events, and has absolutely no fear in strange places, which makes him ideal in any of our outside demonstrations.

He is now coming up to five-years old and seems to get better and better with each year. He is handsome, powerful, intelligent and trustworthy.

More than anything, he symbolizes the start of my journey, both personally and professionally, and a huge portion of my heart belongs to Fortune, and to he alone. I hope that our bond will continue to grow, and that there will be many other critters caught in his lifetime, as part of our hunting expeditions. So he's done well for a "Not a Harris Hawk".

Chapter 10

DIZZY

Dizzy was the first owlet born at Coda Falconry - her parents were a pair of rescued barn owls, which had been given to us. After months of waiting, they decided to breed and give us the gift that was Dizzy (and her brother, Dusk).

After watching three decidedly ugly chicks writhing about in their nest box for ten days, it was now time to put closed rings on the owlets and start the imprinting process, before they grew too big for the ring to fit.

Young birds of prey, including owls, grow at an incredible rate - the difference between a twelve-day old chick and a fourteen-day old chick is a great one. If the closed ring is not slipped over the foot at the optimum age of ten days, it can leave you in a real pickle – attach it too soon and the ring slips off; too late and the ring will simply not go over the foot. You must put a closed ring on a native species of bird before you can sell it or, indeed, just to display it to the public. So, after removing the three chicks from the nest box, they were ringed and placed in a brooder.

At this age, they are blind - barn owls do not tend to open their eyes until they are around thirteen days old. They really are quite hideous to look at: pink, naked and with huge ear cavities on full display; a baby barn owl is not something you would enter into a "cutest baby" competition.

They are also completely vulnerable, and require very specialist care, constant love and attention, if they are to survive this tender stage of their lives.

So, here they were - the very first clutch in my care, all ringed, fed and put in a brooder, with a very fetching white, fluffy hat to sit on. Now the hard work begins.

Barn owl chicks call almost constantly, and you soon begin to realize what each different noise signifies; they emit a very quiet chirping call when they sense you near them, and this chirping call is intensified if they are in any way cold. When they are hungry... boy, do they let you know?! The delicate chirping noises give way to a harsh shrieking sound, which is relentless, until you put the food in their open beaks.

Soon, my three youngsters were growing from ugly, naked things into absolutely beautiful white pom-poms, with heart-shaped facial discs. By four-weeks old, all three barn owl chicks were clambering out of their pen and getting up to all sorts of mischief. At this age the spots start to appear on the underside of the wings, and the chest, if the bird is female (you have to look for these, underneath the fluff); they will remain pure white, with pale back and tail feathers, if the bird is male.[4]

We had two females and one male in this clutch, so I decided to keep a boy and a girl, to show the differences in colour variation between the sexes, when doing my educational visits.

The other female was to be sold to a friend of mine and, by five weeks old, the little female was picked up, and was off to live a grand life at another centre. At the same time I gained Dizzy and Dusk, I had also just picked up a five-week old tawny owl, so I was able to raise all three together, in a very odd looking family.

Dizzy was always the dominant female, and would constantly stretch her wings, right out over her outstretched legs, before bouncing and flapping her way up many obstacles, until she was sat right at the top. Be it a pile of clothes, a chair or a piano, Dizzy had mastered the flap and climb, and was constantly having to be "moved" from her new perches, back to her pen. Inevitably, Dizzy would then wait around five minutes, before escaping to repeat her climbing escapades all over again.

By eleven weeks old, my beautiful Dizzy was really coming into her own. The white fluff gave way to sandy yellows, beiges and blues on the back, and stunning white feathers on her front were speckled with little, chocolate-coloured spots.

Barn owl feathers look like they have been hand-painted - delicate flecks of black and white adorn the canvas of blues and beiges, so it almost looks like they have little strawberry pips, running down each feather. The only thing to top the markings is the sheer softness of the adult feathers; barn owl feathers feel almost cotton-wool-like - they are, without a doubt, the softest feathers of any bird I know of (bar potentially the Great Grey Owl), and this softness, of course, helps them in their efforts to fly silently through the night sky. The edges of each wing have an extremely fine "toothcomb" structure, which reduces any loud turbulence during flight, and the soft, dense plumage absorbs other sounds they make as they fly.

Even at a very young age, Dizzy exuded confidence. When I took her out to an educational visit off-site, or if she came anywhere on displays, she would survey her new surroundings for all-of a few minutes, and then boom: she was off!
Her head would bob from side to side, then she would go one better and completely rotate her face, around 180-degrees, so that her eyes were now where her chin used to be.
She was gathering acoustic information, which allowed her to virtually map her environment, using sound-waves alone.

Barn owls have very acute hearing, and are, basically, sound-wave processing units.
The large, heart-shaped facial disc which surrounds a barn owl's face acts like a "third ear", which is used to magnify and channel sound to its ears - located just behind the facial disc.
Unlike human ears, barn owls actually have one ear higher than the other, so that they can

locate and process sound-waves at different levels and intensities, which helps them fill the niche that no other bird can: they can find prey in the dead of night.

Barn owls are also blessed with incredible long vision, as if they view the world through binoculars. Because their eyes take up a huge amount of space in their skull, and because the eye itself is shaped like an ice cream cone instead of being round, they do not have room in their head for muscles to move them – instead, they have extra vertebrae in their neck, which allows them to turn their head around 270-degrees, in either direction so they have no need to move their eyes.

With a bob and a twist of her head, once Dizzy was satisfied that everything was okay, she would instantly go into explore mode. She would potter up to children, who would be seated in a circle around me, then, as soon as she was directly in front of them, she would repeat her head bobbing and let out a loud, shrieking call, to say "hello" to her newfound friend.
Her brother, Dusk, on the other hand, was a different story.

Each bird has its own personality. Unlike Dizzy, Dusk was shy and more nervous, even though they had been raised together, in exactly the same conditions. Whilst Dizzy was off, taking charge of the entire event, Dusk would follow his sister, to a point (about two-feet of distance, to be exact) and then turn around and make a break for his mum - which was me.

As I was usually sat on the floor, this meant a rather comical flap and dive situation - Dusk had very little wing/foot co-ordination, and would hit me, full pelt, at the end of his clambering, flapping run, flipping himself over my legs and landing, head-first, in my lap. There he would stay, peeping up at me with his large, dark eyes, thinking: It's okay, Mum - let Dizzy take this one.

As Dizzy matured, she really did grow into a gorgeous lady. Her speckles were very defined, along her chest, and her back colouration was mainly a lovely dark blue. She was a fair size for a young female, too: her flying weight was eleven ounces, and because we had started training her to locate her food to a whistle, from a very early age, Dizzy was ready to fly free, as soon as her broad wings could carry her.

*

So, her first day of flight school arrived, and I tied the creance to her jesses and swivel. Dizzy was already calling out to me, in her usual dulcet tones, so, after weighing her, logging the weight and gauging her general behaviour, I could tell that she was ready.

I put her on a perch in the flying arena and walked about ten-feet away from her. I reached into my flying jacket, to bring out a piece of meat to tempt Dizzy, but I did not need it: as I turned to face her, Dizzy crouched down on the perch, flattened all of her feathers, and, with another shriek, she had launched herself clumsily into the air, and was making her way to me. Dizzy wiggled her bum and flapped her wings erratically, before managing to take off. Once in the air, she focused on me entirely.

She did, mercifully, stall above my glove, hover for a few seconds, then: plop! She had landed on my glove, which she now clung to for dear life.

I had to walk her back to the perch the first few times, so that she knew where she had to get to, and to build her confidence, but, before long, Dizzy was flying the full length of the creance, to the perch and to the glove; after two weeks, she was ready to fly free.

Very quickly, Dizzy was "following on" - this is when the bird is watching where you are going, and in which direction you are walking, then takes flight past you, to land on a perch in front of you. It takes an amazing amount of trust, because, basically, the bird you are flying understands that you are its entire focus, and wants to follow you to a position where it can land, keep an eye on its human, but still retain a little independence with the flight.

I loved taking Dizzy for a fly through the Lee Valley Park. Here, we would make our way through the winding footpaths, until we reached the end of the woods, and the trees gave way to another large meadow, with a pond at its centre.

This is a place where she can fly through wild areas and exhibit her natural behaviour in an environment that was made for her; Dizzy loves gliding over the pond, and would pounce on the bull-rushes when they were in bloom. I know that wherever Dizzy ventures to, she will return to me, once I whistle and raise my hand.

We have turned Dizzy's love for flying in the meadows into an experience-day in itself - people who come for our "Owl Encounter" are treated to a woodland walk with Dizzy and, needless to say, they are a great success, with rave reviews from our customers.

As well as being the queen of experience days, Dizzy is also gaining fame in other areas: she has been used in two music videos, by well-known musicians, and has been requested for wildlife photography sessions and night-time photo-shoots, all of which she takes in her stride.

With her 100% success rate in everything she does, we began to open up and trust her as much as she trusted us - another very important job with which we entrust Dizzy is delivering wedding rings to the best-man, as part of a couple's wedding ceremony!

So far, Dizzy has made several brides very happy indeed, by elegantly flying along the aisle and delivering a tiny little bag, filled with the bejewelled rings, ready for the excited couple to take their vows.

I love being a part of people's weddings; we have turned up at a variety of locations, from churches to castles, and even golf clubs, to perform our very special delivery job with Dizzy, and one thing is always the same: a fantastic atmosphere.

Whether the guests know beforehand, or not, about the barn owl ring delivery, as soon as they see Dizzy soaring towards the altar, they are ecstatic, and the cameras don't stop clicking.

The rings are then taken from her anklet and we call her back to us. It really is a wonderful spectacle and event to be representing, and, from all the smiling faces we see looking at us, as their gaze follows Dizzy, we know we really make a positive impact on those people's lives, if just for that one moment.

Dizzy is also the perfect candidate for any of our conservation jobs, as people love seeing a barn owl up close - it really brings home to them just how essential it is to preserve this native species for the next generation. We discuss barn owl nest boxes and environmental controls, which can help encourage them and their prey to visit the area; without a doubt, we find more people are inclined to listen to the information we have given if they get the added bonus of actually seeing a barn owl - it brings reality to conservation.

She is an ambassador for her wild cousins, and a free-flying beauty, bringing so much light into so many people's days. Wherever her wings take her, she knows she has a home waiting for her, and nothing makes me happier than saying that home is with me.

Today, Dizzy is still the same: an amazing young lady. In captivity, barn owls can live up to twenty years, so Dizzy will be a familiar feature at Coda Falconry, for many years to come.

As I watch her lazily taking in the final rays of sunshine in the dying light of the day, eyes closed and standing on one leg in her aviary I can't help but think how lucky I am to have her as part of my flying team.

Ever dependable, she has no idea as she takes flight every day just how important her life is.

Chapter 11

OTIS

Little Otis has been a good friend of mine for just over six years, from when I first decided to take him home with me, from Scotland, following the closure of one of my friends' centres. He, along with a few other birds, is the true foundation of Coda Falconry, and I was grateful for the opportunity to rehouse all of these beautiful birds, and to give them the best life I could in their new home.

Otis is a Sunda scops owl. Not much is known about this tiny, strictly nocturnal species of owl, despite it being incredibly common in its homeland of Malaysia and Indonesia. Of the forty-five recognized species of scops owls in the world, the Sunda scops is one of the few actually benefitting from humanization; they have now been spotted making their nests in buildings, as well as tree hollows, which means that this species is very adaptive to change.[5]

Of course, where there are humans, there is a lot of rubbish, but, again, the Sundas are capitalizing on this opportunity - these owls are almost entirely insectivorous (which means they eat a huge variety of insects, beetles and arachnids, as the staple part of their diet), and Sunda scops owls pick off the insects living on and around humans' rubbish.

It is a small, adaptive owl, with a very distinctive

call.

At only five ounces in weight, and standing at a whopping six-inches tall, with just over a ten-inch wingspan, Otis does not cut a very imposing form. Add to this his beautiful camouflage of mottled browns, blacks and white flecks, and, believe me, you could easily lose him against the background.

There was a gentle shyness which overshadowed Otis. He was not what you would call a "sociable" bird - he looked a little sorry for himself, after the long drive home from Scotland, and due to his tiny size, and not very hardy nature, it was decided that he would stay inside with us, in his very own enclosure, so that he could have a constant room temperature, and get used to being socialized again.

As a general rule of thumb, the smaller the bird of prey, the harder it is to maintain good weight control.

It is very easy to underfeed a bird which only weighs five ounces - birds of prey have a high metabolic rate, and a fast beat to their heart, so if they do not gain enough energy from the food going in, you run the risk of the smaller birds dropping weight too quickly, and, eventually, this will cost them their life.

With some of the smaller birds, half an ounce either side of their flying weight can be the difference between the bird collapsing from starvation or, at the other end of the scale, being too fat to recall when flying them free. In the wild, Sunda scops owls conserve a lot of their energy by not doing an awful lot of flying - this species prefers to hop and flutter through the branches of trees, picking off insects as it goes. Otis was no exception – at just over four ounces, he would hop to his food; any lower than that, he would be in trouble, while at 5.5oz., Otis would sit there like a chubby potato. We used to allow him to fly down our stairs when we were there, so that he could get as much exercise as possible.

Otis is one of the species of owls which does not have silent flight - when he flaps his wings, with his indelicate and erratic flapping motions, he makes the most heavy "whooshing" noises.

We kept a note of his behaviour throughout the week; as he was so small, it was very important to keep an eye on his weight and make sure that he was eating well and in good condition, following his long journey.

"Day 1: not much to report, really. Otis continues to sit in the corner of the living room, staring at us like an emotionless, winged super-villain. Fed him a mouse. He took the mouse from my hand, slowly grasping it with his outstretched right foot, then slinked away to the back of his enclosure to eat it. Slightly sinister.

"Day 2, 3, 4 and 5 - same as day 1.

"Day 6 - something is changing."

It started when we were watching TV. Out of the corner of my eye, I saw a little, potato-shaped object suddenly appear by my left shoulder - I turned to find Otis, perched on the back of the sofa.

"Hello buddy!" was the only thing I could think to say.

Otis let out a very hearty "WHOOOP!" in response.

I let him sit there all night with me. He took in what was going on around him, and seemed to make some quiet purring noises, between the more triumphant whoops - it became clear he was starting to settle in nicely.

Boy, could he pack the food away!? He was eating two mice per day, or one whole chick - not far off of what I feed my barn owls, which are twice his size! So, it was also clear that his appetite was healthy.

For the next couple of weeks, we allowed Otis to mooch around our home, and included him in our day-to-day activities. We really started to get to know the true character of this owl: Otis began to love attention.

Sunda scops owls have tiny, whisker-like bristles around the base of their beaks. These bristles are very sensitive to touch, and are used by the birds to feel around at close range, so they can locate food or obstructions in their local environment, and avoid collisions, as they navigate through the branches of trees at night.

But, Otis – he just wanted his to be stroked. I reached out to touch him one night and, after initially backing away, he lowered his head, closed his eyes and pushed his bristly beak onto my outstretched finger - I started to stroke around his beak and he nudged further towards me. I continued to fuss him for a good ten minutes, running my finger around to the side of his head, as he gently turned his head to present the spot he wanted massaged.

As I said before: Otis loves attention. We continued to work with and socialize Otis, throughout the winter. Soon, he began actively seeking out human company, and would sit on my laptop at work, making his peculiar little bubbling purr noises at me - I responded with noises back to him. Otis moved into his new aviary in the summer months.

Sunda scops owls are designed to stay as hidden as possible – it is the only way they can avoid the huge number of predators which would like to have them as a snack – so, we made sure he felt comfortable in his own home, by providing a variety of hidey-holes, and branches for him to rest against, during the day.

Throughout the following years, Otis really thrived - he moulted out his tatty, broken tail and really does look like a very handsome chap indeed, now.

He has a regular routine, too: he always has the biggest bath possible, right before an experience-day in which he is to be involved, so that he looks as much like a drowned rat as possible, for his adoring guests.

I think that of all the birds at Coda Falconry, Otis has really lightened the most hearts. Children of all ages and abilities are able to get close to him, and his kind, attentive nature really enhances their experience of being up close to an owl. Adults also queue up, just to see him, when we do our outside events.

Otis has his own fan club, and is requested at many of our events and photography days; this is no surprise really, because his plumage is absolutely stunning - when we pop him into a tree, to give the "natural look" that so many of our photography guests like, the results are incredible: his feathers contrast and blend into the wood like a masterpiece, and his beautiful, dark-brown eyes are usually covered by his long eyelashes, as he lazily stares out onto the wide, expanding world around him.

One of the jobs that we used Otis for was at a local Alzheimer's care-home. The carers had briefed me beforehand that some of the residents could be aggressive, due to their advanced onset of Alzheimer's disease, and that they would gauge whether or not it was feasible for those residents to engage with the owls.

I did not know much about Alzheimer's disease at all, prior to our visit - I am very fortunate in that none of my friends or family have ever suffered with this illness.

However, with my limited understanding, I had just assumed that the disease affected memory, and that patients would have difficulty remembering parts of their life. I learnt from the carers and doctors on-site that Alzheimer's disease actually affects not only memory loss, but also problem-solving, language and moods.

Alzheimer's disease is caused when proteins build up in the brain and cause a loss of connection between nerve cells - this leads to a loss of brain tissue, over time. There are more than 520,000 people in the UK with Alzheimer's disease and, unfortunately, it is a progressive disease, which means that gradually, over time, the symptoms become more severe; there is no known cure.[6]

We were taken through to the communal lounge, where an eager group of residents and their families had gathered to hear a talk which I was scheduled to give, on owls. I introduced myself and my colleague to the group, and we started with a nice, informal discussion about the owls at our centre, and the owl that we had brought along to show them this afternoon. As I opened the door to a tiny, little travel-box, which I had left in the corner of the room, you could almost feel the excitement in the atmosphere growing: everyone in the room was waiting to see what was hiding inside.

Out came Otis.

Gasps filled the room, along with:

"Oh, he's a little darling…"

"What a cute little owl…"

..a whole murmuring of positive and beautiful sentiments surrounded us.

Otis looked around at his adoring fans, then closed his eyes and settled on my glove. We visited each of the residents and their families in turn; the carers were thrilled that even the patients with very severe cases of Alzheimer's disease seemed to shine from within. There was no hint of aggressive behaviour from anyone, and I was happy to let them reach out a finger and stroke our delicate little Sunda scops owl.

I explained to everyone how old he was, what he liked to eat, his name and what species of owl he was.

Many of the residents had tears in their eyes - they just could not believe that they were in the presence of this owl, and not only that, but that they could learn about him, and actually interact with our little Otis (who, of course, was lapping up the attention, as usual).

Expressions of sheer delight filled the communal lounge, and with each finger held out to him, Otis would press his head forward against the instrument of stroking heaven, and nuzzle into the hands, with great affection.

At the end of the talk, I asked if everyone had enjoyed their visit from Otis, and it was clear from their responses that this had meant the world to all of them. I took a few questions from the family members of some of the residents, which I was enthusiastically answering, when, all of a sudden, a patient put up her hand.

The carer who was looking after this lady said: "This is Lynn - she's been here a while."

I walked over, knelt down in front of her and said: "Hi Lynn, it's lovely to meet you - is this your family?" She was surrounded by her son, daughter-in-law and their two children, who introduced themselves to me, as Lynn could not speak very well.

Her carer went on to say: "Sorry, she only has a ten-minute memory - she can't remember anything over that time. But, we all really enjoyed seeing the owl."

In almost total defiance of the rule book, Lynn then took my hand and said, in a very quiet voice: "Otis - scops owl."

I had given my talk and the information on Otis roughly thirty minutes prior to meeting her; given the fact that normally she could not remember anything after ten minutes, this was monumental - her son got up out of his chair and gave me a hug! This was a real eye-opener to how important my job could be, and I knew that I would cherish that moment for the rest of my life.

Otis had managed to break down barriers in the minds of severely ill human-beings, and allowed them to reflect on their memories, if only for just a brief moment.

I also owe a lot to Otis.

He is so very loved and treasured not just by me, but by my whole team, family and well quite frankly, anyone who has had the pleasure of his company.

As he's been there from the very start, Otis has seen me through the darkest times of my business, when all of the world seemed to be outside ready and waiting to pounce on me, this little Sunda scops owl was always there with no malice in his entire being. His only wants were to be safe, well fed and doted upon. There would be a time I surmised when I would look back and realise that all the hardships were just paving the way for the good times and that it would be worth fighting for.

Otis taught me a lot in those early days about sticking to your guns and defending what you believe in – his development and trust in me was worth protecting.

If I gave up, he might not have a home. Just a tiny raindrop in a desert can be enough to make a seed grow and so it was with my relationship with this Sunda scops owl.

He gave me something to believe in and from that roots could grow and a business was born.

Chapter 12

POPPY

I had wanted a Harris hawk for my new centre because, in the right hands, they are absolutely magnificent birds of prey - they are very successful hunters and their obedient, sociable nature means that they are quick to learn and happy to fly to a variety of people; they are a good all-rounder. For a falconry centre which runs experience-days, flying demonstrations and educational visits, all of these things are very much appreciated.

As luck would have it, the same breeder who bred my beautiful red-tailed buzzard, Fortune, also had a breeding pair of Harris hawks, which had just hatched a lonely egg and were not particularly fussed about caring for the chick, as it was coming into mid-winter and, quite frankly, the little chick was a mistake. This lonely Harris hawk egg had hatched into Poppy, who was only two weeks old when I got her.

When I saw Poppy, I knew that this little, cream-coloured bundle of fluff was going to come home with me.

At this point, we were all unsure of what sex she would be – obviously, when so young it is difficult to know for sure, until the chick starts to grow. Female Harris hawks are roughly one-third bigger than males, and are much more dominant in character; this chick did have absolutely huge feet, so I sort of guessed it was going to be a female, and I would place my bets on that, until I knew for sure.

Naming a bird of prey has always been a bit of a challenge for me - I hate cliché names, or ones which scream ego, so I generally try to pick a name which is meaningful to me, to the country of origin, or to the character of the bird. It was near to Remembrance Sunday when I picked up this little fluff-ball, so I decided to call her "Poppy".

Harris hawks are, without a doubt, the most popular bird of prey used in falconry today; they are unique amongst raptors, because they are a sociable bird.

They originate from South America and inhabit the deserts of these countries, so what you have is a sleek, large predator, which is capable of survival in some very extreme environments.

In order to maximize survival, the Harris hawk lives in family groups of up to seven individual birds - these groups are called "casts".

I drove her back home (I was staying with my mum at the time) in a tiny little biscuit box carrier, and she was very laid back about the whole thing.

Whenever we stopped at traffic lights, little Poppy would start chirping loudly, completely oblivious to the whirling world of flashing lights and noise which surrounded her. Her dark eyes would focus on an object and let it catch her imagination for a fleeting few seconds; in order to fully grasp these interesting moments, Poppy would turn her head 180-degrees, so that it looked like it was stuck on upside-down, which was, quite frankly, a little unnerving. Poppy took the journey home in her stride and, within an hour, I walked through the front door with a new family member.

One special superpower Poppy had - which I didn't realize until I got her home - was that she could actually poop about three-feet in any direction! Newspaper became more precious than gold in our house, while Poppy was growing up, and even the neighbours chipped in, leaving bags of old papers on our front doorstep.

We moved her into a Moses basket, with layers of warm, soft blankets, so she had a VIP nest, which she could snuggle into when she was tired.

Soon, our little fluffy bundle began to sprout feathers on her wings and tail (these tend to grow first on birds of prey), though Poppy was still very wobbly on her feet, and could only really stand up when she was flapping her wings - after the frantic wing beats, she would slump back down, onto her folded legs, and think about what she had just done.

One day Poppy decided that the world outside of her basket was just too interesting to ignore any more. With a flurry of wings and legs scrambling, she was airborne - and heading straight for my mum. Poppy was around six weeks old now, and about the same shape and density as a feral pigeon.

Poppy had a clear target: that was Mum's head; Mum also had a clear view of what was about to happen.

With a mug of tea in her hand, she displayed an astonishing ability to "Keep calm and carry on" and with what appeared to me like a slow motion action scene in a movie, Poppy crossed the living room, having flown around ten-feet, just so that she could alight on Mum's waiting scalp.

I could tell that Poppy was delighted with herself - she stomped around on this new, warm landing-post, flapping her wings to keep balance, as she explored the hair follicles, which she now found herself amongst.

Mum was not as delighted - she stayed put, like a statue, throughout the whole hawk ordeal and, as Mum's eyes were firmly closed, I was ordered to remove the bird.

Quite remarkably, the mug of tea stayed intact with not one drop spilt.

From this point forward, Poppy was well on the move. She grew up so fast and, by four months old, we had a little lady hawk, all-feathered and full of energy, striking an elegant and regal pose, whenever she stood tall on her various perches. From now on, Poppy was teaching me what it was to be a Harris hawk.

Being a social animal, Harris hawks communicate in a similar way to any other pack animal - they have their own form of a vocal "language", as well as tail wags/flicks and gesturing with their wings.

When young birds are forming their hierarchy within the cast, it is not uncommon to see two or more Harris hawks, with wings outstretched right above their back, heads bowed in a threatening stance, feet primed and ready to strike.

Normally, there is a lot of screaming which accompanies this particular show-off routine and, after an exchange of vocalizations, usually the more submissive hawk will back down.

If the two Harris hawks are more evenly matched, however, they will lash out with their long legs and powerful feet; normally, both will strike at a similar time, which leads to their locking feet together in an unshakeable grasp, until one has had enough and admits defeat.

These fights however, can result in the death of one or both parties, due to injuries sustained from the talons; so, in the main, Harris hawks are "more mouth than trouser" with one another, and despite a few arguments amongst the teenagers of the cast, the Harris hawk is well known for having a gregarious and personable nature, co-existing with its own kind, in order to maximise the species' success in hunting.

It is important to understand how integral their social etiquettes are, when raising a young

Harris hawk, because all of these lessons need to be taught by the parents at a young age, and you are effectively the young hawk's parent - they will look to you for everything they need: food, water, shelter and comfort, along with a whole array of life lessons, which they will just assume you know.

The young bird will also look to you for discipline.

Obviously, as a falconer, it is wicked and unfathomable to strike your bird of prey - anyone within the "falconry" community who does so should be hit back, just as hard, and have their birds taken away from them. Still, when Poppy challenged me, I had to discipline her, so that she would know that I was the "alpha" within her cast. I simply took a firm hold of her, sandwiched her wriggly mass between my knees, and sat on her - well, sort of squatted over her, would perhaps be the more accurate term. After about thirty seconds, her growls became submissive cheeps, and, as soon as that was vocalized, I stood up.

Poppy shuffled away - a little indignant, but the message was well and truly read, loud and clear; she never challenged me again after this.

These lessons are important, as, when a Harris hawk grows up, he or she will have a lot of physical power behind them, and a lot of brain-power to back it up.

If a Harris hawk thinks that you are beneath it in the hierarchy, then you are in big trouble - it will be aggressive towards you, totally ignorant to your command, and suddenly there will be a two-pound-plus flying predator swooping around, with no fear or respect for human-beings, and an inflated opinion of itself.

That is when you start seeing injuries to people's faces and hands; Harris hawks can and will take any action which makes them unpredictable and dangerous.

So, see?

It is a BIG responsibility raising a young raptor.

As she got bigger, and into her full, juvenile plumage, Poppy was incredibly loyal, but also very adventurous.

She now weighed in at two-pounds and was fully grown, despite the fact that she still needed to bulk out a little - as she had not really flown much, her flight muscles needed developing, which was exactly what I started to work on.

I do love Harris hawks in their juvenile plumage - they have light-beige flecks, running all the way down their body, and the most stunning "zebra" stripe pattern on the underside of their tails; they are a beautiful concoction of brown, beige, black, white and a washed-out russet-red, and are an amazing sight to behold.

On the day of her first flight training session, Poppy stood tall on her perch, which was situated in the flying arena at Coda Falconry; she was a maturing beauty now, with all of her falconry equipment on, and she glistened in the mid-morning sun.

"Okay, let's see what you can do then, missus!" was my pep-talk for the day.

I had tied the creance to her swivel and chopped up enough food for her daily allowance.

Obviously, at this stage, you do not know what the correct flying weight of your bird is – that is where the creance comes in. If a bird of prey you are training is not responsive to food, it means you need to cut their weight a little; if a bird of prey is overweight, it simply will not do anything (just like its wild cousins), so, in order to get a bird focused in these early stages, food is the answer. Without a creance, you could potentially be letting an untrained bird, which is too heavy, loose in the world, and you would have no hope of getting it back. So, the creance usually stays on the trainee, until the bird can be recalled a fair way - usually the entire length of the creance - just to make sure that the training is ingrained, and decrease likelihood that the young bird will go off on a wander.

I had already been feeding Poppy on my glove, then making her jump to my glove when she was getting confident of what she had to do, so the basics had been started.

Being an imprint, she had a very tight bond with me and, like a new puppy, she did not want to be too far from my side; I knew that this would mean her training period was likely to be very short indeed - she already knew that I was the food provider, and her sociable nature meant that she saw herself as part of my team, so it was doubtful that she would go far at all.

As expected, Poppy was phenomenal.

She was a chatterbox, that's for sure (as most imprints are), and she decided to call to me from the minute she was on the perch, right the way through her flight, and then continue to chatter to me on the glove, before realizing that she needed to be quiet, in order to eat her food.

I did ten recalls that day, and finished the flight training with a big piece of skinned rabbit leg, so Poppy understood that coming back meant a huge reward. She filled her crop, and I popped her back into her aviary, ready for more flight training the next day.

Before long, Poppy was flying free in the arena, and also doing some incredible flights, out in the woodlands which backed on to our centre. She was becoming quicker in flight, and so fit that she could bank up, almost vertically, onto telegraph poles which lined the footpaths where we went to fly the birds.

I started using Poppy on our experience-days, and also our public flying demonstrations.

Her sweet nature just blossomed, the older she became - you could pick her up like a chicken, and she would actively seek out warmth on cold, winter displays, by waddling up to whoever was near and "pipping" gently at their feet, as if to say: "please pick me up".

Then, once her big, brown eyes had won the poor, unsuspecting display falconer over, and she was safely on their lap, Poppy would dive down inside their jumper, and poke her head out of the half-open zip - there she would undoubtedly stay, until such time as she was warm enough again.

Poppy was one of the most gentle raptors I have ever known, and I fell in love with her the more I flew and got to know her.

She was also a real comedian: if you were holding anything in your right hand, with her on the glove, she was into it!

I lost count of the amount of times she flung arena maps out of my hand and onto the floor (much to the amusement of the general public), and if you put your handbag down, she would jump inside it, like a chihuahua, and turf out all the little trinkets she could find in there. I started packing less personal items in my handbags, from that moment on.

With children, you could not have asked for a better bird of prey for them to handle. I am not usually one to allow kids to handle larger birds of prey, because they do not have a lot of strength in their arms, and the wingspans of some of our birds can actually be larger than them, so it can become a bit awkward trying to land a bird of that size on a small person's arm.

If, however, you were with a child that really wanted to fly a hawk, Poppy would be called upon - with zero aggression, no desire to hunt and a peaceful nature, she excelled at thrilling people of all ages; without a doubt, I saw a "grand display and experience-day" bird in her.

Things, however, changed, one fateful day. As with all things in nature, the unexpected can happen, which totally wipes the slate clean and forces you to rethink your entire plans.

Poppy was just coming into her second year, and she was a force to be reckoned with - she soared like a buzzard, on thermals, and was ultra-fit. I was flying her to an experience-day guest, as I had been for the past year, when, all of a sudden, something was not right with the way Poppy was behaving - she seemed distant and agitated. I tried to recall her several times, but to no avail, before, totally out of character, Poppy shot off like a rocket, in the opposite direction to where we were. She flew low, fast and deliberately towards a fixed point, then disappeared out of sight, to the bottom of the hill where we were standing.

All I heard next was a blood-curdling scream, and at that, me and the guests (who absolutely wanted to know what was going on and would not leave my side) ran across to where the noise was coming from, and located Poppy on the floor, in a mantle position.

Her back and head feathers were puffed out, and her wings were dropped over something, which was still wriggling in her feet.

An instant feeling of relief swept over me - Poppy was unhurt - as the reason for her moment of aloofness became clear: she had seen a large rabbit, in the field next door, and had wanted to try out her hunting skills.

Our guests were delighted - they were now

having the authentic falconry experience, as here was a young Harris hawk, gripping tightly to the head and body of a rabbit and behaving exactly as she would in the wild.

I knelt down next to her, and the poor rabbit which had found itself on her dinner menu. Birds of prey are cruel when it comes to their food, and will start eating their catch while it is still alive, so, as a falconer, it is important to dispatch (kill) the animal that they have caught, in order to put it out of its misery, as soon as possible. Once this was done, I let Poppy pluck at her prize and eat a small amount of the rabbit as a reward.

At this point, another thought crossed my mind: I had heard, that apparently, when imprints start hunting they turn nasty towards their handler, and pretty much bugger off, to become self-sufficient.

So, instead of being a generic experience-day bird, which flew at the centre, Poppy needed a role change. The meerkat enclosure had been moved next to the bird of prey flying arena, so this kind of buggered things up for the birds more likely to hunt small, furry animals - after a team briefing, it was decided that all the birds capable of catching meerkats had to be flown off-site; due to her rabbit killing debut, Poppy was put into this category, as I would rather be safe than sorry.

It was a good call on my behalf - to say that she excelled as a hunting bird would be rather an understatement! To date, Poppy has caught greylag geese, ducks (much to my despair, as I love ducks), moor-hens, herring-gulls, rabbits, rats (yuk!), mice, and has a particular fondness for chasing and killing wood-pigeons. I take Poppy out with me, to my pest-control sites, so she can blast into the gulls and scare them away, and she is still the bird I use most often on my outside flying and static demonstrations.

Poppy is now an immaculate adult. Her juvenile plumage has given way to rich chocolate-browns, blacks and two deep-red patches on each wing.

If you have had an experience-day at Coda Falconry, you will have met Poppy, if not as part of the flying experience, then certainly as part of the introduction to our centre. She is my baby; I can work with her all day, and know exactly how she is feeling and where she wants to go.

Poppy has never challenged me; she has never shown aggression - she calls out only when she sees me, or has perceived danger (usually a dog!), and has retained her playful personality, despite being the best hunting bird I have ever had. Reliable, loyal and dependable, Poppy is all you would ever need, if you were just going to keep one bird to hunt with.

When I publicised on my website that I had a baby harris hawk that I was going to imprint, some people started saying negative things about how imprint Harris hawks were aggressive towards their handlers and terrible at hunting – how I would ruin a good bird by raising her in this way.

She proved them wrong and I was merely the scribe that could see this beautiful story unfurling - I was so pleased that I chose to take a chance on a wild card.

Everything that the doubters shouted our way faded to dust when this astonishing female imprint Harris hawk took to the skies and outshone their hawks with embarrassing ease.

I grew in confidence because of her. We learnt together that everyone is an individual whether you are a human or a raptor and to believe only what you see in front of you not the rumours.

I tell our story to anyone who wishes to listen because I think it's important to realise that we all have room to grow and improve but taking a chance on something you love will make you a better person in the end. That's what Poppy has taught me.

I wish I could tell her in her own language just how much she means to me and how my life would be so different without her.

She came to me at the exact moment I needed her the most and for that, I am truly grateful.

*

Harris hawks are sadly dubbed "the beginner's bird", because most people new to the sport of falconry end up buying one of them.

But, they are not a beginner's bird; there is no such thing as a beginner's bird,

In order to raise and train a healthy, well-balanced bird of prey, to fly free and eventually hunt with you, you need experience, whether that is gained volunteering at a falconry centre, or working alongside a falconer, who is prepared to share his/her knowledge with you.

It is imperative, for the sake of you and your bird, that you at least know the essentials of how to look after this new life, which will come to depend on you for food, shelter, friendship, trust and... well, everything!

Due to the Harris hawk's popularity, unscrupulous breeders started popping up all over the country, trying to cash in on the insurgence of people which were looking for this species to own. That, in turn, leads to inbreeding, the inevitable result of which is unhealthy offspring.

I don't know why there are so many Harris hawks currently floating about in the UK, without a falconer friend to call them in, and I get tired of seeing reports about yet another Harris hawk, spotted living wild, and the poor thing has not even been reported as missing. Our sad, throw-away culture unfortunately reaches to birds of prey, too, and the Harris hawk, being so popular, has had to bear the brunt of this ignorance. Let us hope that the tides can change, and that the Harris hawk can go back to being an incredible falconry bird, when in the right hands - not just the "beginner's" bird.

Chapter 13

LOGAN

Eurasian eagle-owls are gigantic, beautiful owls, which are lazy, laid back and usually very friendly. Their soft, thick plumage creates layer upon layer of insulated cover on their impressive bodies and, even in the coldest climates,

Eurasian eagle-owls thrive as the apex predators of the skies.

The Eurasian eagle-owl can be found across much of Europe, the Middle East, Russia and Asia.

Eurasian eagle-owls were once resident in the UK, but the species died out in this country around the Mesolithic era (circa 9,000–10,000 years ago), and wild populations were never recorded until more recently.

New research indicates that, during the Mesolithic era, there was a land bridge connecting Britain to mainland Europe, so the eagle-owls could quite easily cross over to our country, without the need to make the long flight over a mass of water.

As this land flooded with water, and became the Channel, as we know it today, it became more perilous for an eagle-owl to cross, so there was an isolated number of this species left on our little island, while the rest of the population stayed put, on Europe's mainland.[7]

Small numbers are now beginning to breed in Britain again.

riginally, it was thought that these were derived from escaped captive birds; however, after following the migratory paths of Eurasian eagle-owl populations in northern Europe, distances as long as four-hundred miles have been recorded, so it is very feasible that our recent population of Eurasian eagle-owls has descended from individuals, which crossed from Scandinavia and western Europe, as a perfectly natural migratory path.

They eat a huge variety of prey – rodents, such as voles, mice and rats, as well as rabbits, hares and even carrion, make up a large proportion of their diet; Eurasian eagle-owls have also been known to swoop on buzzards and goshawks, roosting in the branches of trees around dusk - this is when the Eurasian eagle-owl really comes to life.

For a gigantic lump of feathers, weighing in at over four-pounds (eight-pounds in some females), and with a wingspan of well over six-feet, the Eurasian eagle-owl is a surprisingly stealthy predator - if a Eurasian eagle-owl flew over the top of your head, you would not be able to hear it.

Their feathers are typical of most owl species, and are incredibly soft, which reduces any sound made by the mechanics of flight.

Feared by anything smaller, this species of owl really does make an impact on its immediate territory, which is typically around 10km in diameter - when an eagle-owl moves into the area, pretty much any other predator moves out; even the prey species will jostle their position, to try and stay out of those mighty feet.

Along with a natural inclination to hunt in the dark, the Eurasian eagle-owl is the true master of the night.

*

Before the first time I saw Logan, I had visions of a beautiful Eurasian eagle-owl - a force of nature in full adult plumage, with striking eyebrows and a manly hoot.

When he finally arrived, I could not wait to open the bird-box - when I did, two dark-orange eyes peered back at me, from the bottom of the box. There were no gentle shades of brown and black, no swathes of sandy yellow and certainly no funky eyebrows. In the box was a grey ball of fluff, which looked like a Furby.
This was the first encounter with the – then – baby, Logan.

I took him into the living room. My mum had been making tea in the kitchen, and she came and stood next to me, to view our new arrival.
As I opened the lid, once again two orange, marble-like eyes were fixed on us.

"He's huge!" my mum said - until this point, the largest owlet my mum had ever seen was a barn owl.

"No, he's not - he's only six weeks old! He's

actually going to get a lot bigger-" I stopped myself, as I could see the blood draining from Mum's face. "Well, never mind all that - it'll take a while for him to be fully grown. Isn't he cute!?"

My mum looked down at Logan, who was now puffing himself up, to make himself look as big as possible, clacking his beak and hissing.

"Hmmmmm, not really - he seems a little angry," replied my mum. She went to the kitchen to finish making the tea, and leave me alone with the hissing fluff-ball. I hated to admit it but she was right. There were many adjectives that could be used to describe Logan but I think cute was low down on that list.

"Right, come on, you," I said, in my most stern voice, before scooping him up - still hissing – and placing him down on the living-room floor.

He shook himself clear of me and trotted a few steps forward; he began bobbing his head, surveying the immediate area. Then, he began charging around every nook and cranny of the room, to explore. I offered him some mice, as he had not eaten all day, but despite that, he was not hungry.

It was getting late, so I put him in his new owlet pen and let him settle down for the night. The next morning, Logan was bobbing about his pen, as I opened the top to have a look at him.

"Hello, menace," I whispered to him.

He bobbed his head at me, opened up his beak and croaked a very hearty "wheeep!" at me.

"Okay then, my friend," I replied; "well, if

that's us now on talking terms, then we're doing okay."

Now, Logan was hungry - he was [now] an eating machine, munching his way through eight chicks, four mice and a quail! He obviously needed the food because he was growing so quickly.

By twelve weeks old, Logan had developed full flight feathers - his tail and most of his body were feathering, too.

His head lacked the prominent ear tufts, which give this species so much character, but they would come later. One thing he did retain, for a very long time, was the "petticoat" of young down, which hung around his waist and made him look like he was wearing a skirt.

Before his first birthday, Logan was a stunning, adult Eurasian eagle-owl. As part of his first birthday celebration, we got the audience at one of our displays to sing Logan "Happy Birthday", as he sat there, on a post in our flying arena, with his chin up, eyes squinting and white throat-patch puffed out. He responded to his very own applause with his usual "wheep!".

Logan has been rather a handful, throughout the years.

Once, I let Logan fly free, as usual for his time in the arena, and began to tell the audience all about the Eurasian eagle-owl: where they like to live and what they like to eat, etc. Logan decided to take himself off, into a tall oak tree, which sits on the edge of the flying arena.

This was strange, because Logan was the laziest creature I had ever met, and getting him to fly anywhere was usually an ordeal. Logan sat on a branch, looking toward the trunk of the tree, then suddenly leapt from the top branches, swerved around the canopy of the oak and, with about as much finesse as a diving hippo, fell out of the tree and hurtled towards the ground. His wings opened at the very last moment, and he landed with a thud on the ground.

Oh, dear, was my immediate thought. I rushed over to Logan.

He had puffed himself up to almost twice his usual size, and even the feathers on his head, which were usually so flattened and perfect, were sticking up, like a hedgehog's quills. He appeared to be mantling over something, which was in his feet.

"Okay, everyone, it looks like Logan has caught something, so I'm going to end the show here and sort him out. Thank you, everyone, for watching - my colleague is going to speak to you about the other birds, so please do follow him, and he'll give you a guided tour of the centre." Although I tried to get the audience away, so that I could deal with Logan by myself, they were far too curious, and followed me.

As I approached Logan, with the audience following, he puffed out his feathers, as far as they could go, and dropped his wings either side of his body, to make himself look extra huge. Then, he started to hiss and clack his beak; his eyes were bulging, like giant, orange golf balls stuck to his face. Logan obviously wanted me to back off; in any other circumstances I would, but I needed to see what was going on, and to get him back to his usual self.

I slid my gloved hand underneath him and found a solid object between his talons: a dead squirrel - Logan had twisted and turned through the branches, and, with his eyes locked on his target, had caught the grey squirrel completely off-guard.

It was important that Logan did not get to have any of this food, because the last thing I wanted him to do was hunt - as a huge part of our flying and experience-day team, a Eurasian eagle-owl which decides to hunt for itself is not good, and potentially extremely dangerous to dog-walkers in the local area. So, I swapped the dead squirrel for a chick, which I had in my flying vest, then I took the dead squirrel back to the centre.

As I passed the large crowd, people called out: "What was it?"

"Oh, it was a grey squirrel. I'm ever so sorry about that - unfortunately, I can't stop him from doing what his natural instinct tells him to, when he gets the chance. Hey, at least it was an authentic falconry display, right?" I replied, smiling. No one else was smiling back.

I quickly turned and carried on walking to the centre. As I walked away, I heard one of the little girls say: "Daddy, has the squirrel gone to heaven?" Oh the shame!

A short while later, the manager of the farm walked into our office and asked us about our fateful show - I explained that Logan had killed a squirrel.

"What squirrel?" the manager asked, with a worried look on her face.

I stopped giggling. "Erm… a grey squirrel. Why? Is there a particular squirrel that you know of?" I replied, jokingly.

"Oh! I hope it wasn't Cyril! I've hand-reared him from a young age, and he often pops into the office for food."

A sudden feeling of dread swept over me. "Cyril?" I uttered back, in a squeaky voice; "So… what would make this squirrel a Cyril, then?" I was hoping upon hope that whatever Logan had caught was not Cyril.

"Ah, you'd know if it was Cyril," the manager replied: "he's got a cleft-palate, which is probably why he was abandoned at a young age."

I had already "prepped" the grey squirrel carcass and had divided the meat amongst my hunting hawks as fresh meat certainly shouldn't be wasted. I gave the head part to Fortune, my red-tailed buzzard as it's a particular favourite of his.

"Oh, well, I'm sure it wasn't Cyril - it was probably just a youngster, which was easy pickings for Logan - and that little Cyril will be back for his lunch, later."

Both me and Kate stopped outside Fortune's aviary.

Just as I finished my sentence, Fortune turned around to face us, manoeuvred his feet and flopped something from the back of the perch to the front... revealing one grey squirrel's head, with a cleft palate.

I couldn't believe it.

I felt awful.

After Kate had gone back to her office (after several conversations involving me apologising), I walked over to Logan and said "Well thank you very much for one of the most awkward days of my life!"

Logan couldn't' care less - he was far too busy sunning himself on his favourite log after consuming his food.

That was the first and last kill Logan ever made I'm pleased to say and thankfully, no more squirrels have been harmed in the making of our flying displays.

Eagle owls do last a very long time in captivity, there are some individuals that are now well into their 60's so it's a sad fact that Logan will probably outlive me and my team.

I intend to enjoy his company and his humorous behaviour for the rest of my days – I think we will probably grow old and grumpy together.

Despite balloons which for some reason, utterly terrify him, nothing phases our Logan.

We all call him "The Bomber" because he is slow, dependable and steady with his work. Our

"Owl Encounter" guests absolutely love the magical moment of having the largest species of owl in the world land on their glove; Logan is a powerhouse of beauty, grace and pride.

It's good that he has a more aggressive nature than some of our other birds or you might be lured into the false sense of security that the Eurasian eagle owl is a cuddly, cute animal that you see in cartoons instead of an apex predator of dusk and dawn which is a realm that they rule implicitly.

Every year I see darker feathers coming through into Logan's plumage and he is such a huge character to have around so much so that everyone now calls him Lord Logan which I think is very fitting.

Logan draws the biggest crowds and rightly so - he is a grand old thing who absolutely believes that he is the centre of the universe. As Logan is the centre of the Coda Falconry universe, we'll let him get away with that.

Chapter 14

LOKI

Although Coda Falconry is a bird of prey centre, I had been interested in training a raven, which is not a bird of prey.

Ravens are very beautiful.

As the sun shines on its feathers, there are hues of blue and even green - an iridescence which corvids seem to do so well. As the largest member of the corvid (crow) family, the raven does strike a very menacing pose. With a body length of 22-30 inches, and a wingspan of roughly five-feet, this is a large, black bird, with a powerful presence.

Speaking of powerful: that beak!

Easily four-inches long and just over an inch thick at the base, a raven's beak tapers to a sharp point; it can be used for anything from cracking open the shells of nuts, to boring out holes in wood, and right through to other extremes of gently using tools, like twigs, to tease out a tasty morsel, as well as affectionately preening friends.

In 2015, one of my colleagues messaged me, to tell me she had found a raven for sale.

"Apparently, he's only a year old, has been hand-reared and is used to wearing leather equipment."

I sat back and thought about this for a

moment. "Okay, then," I typed back; "let's go and see this raven."

I phoned the breeder, and found that the raven had a rather sad backstory: his previous owner (who had bought him directly from the breeder) had passed away, and, of course, in this ailing health, the raven had not been particularly well looked after.

The raven had then been returned to the breeder, after his owner had passed away.

We met with the breeder, at his house, and were shown into the back garden, where a huge, black figure of a raven loomed on a bow perch, at the side of the garden.

As we approached, the raven looked at us and started a very harsh, deep call in our direction: "Boh! Boh! Boh!" His head looked rather fluffy, as he had gone into full "back off!" mode, and was trying to show us exactly who was boss.

"He's just showing off now," were the words the breeder muttered.

Slightly nervous, I went to have a closer look.

I checked out his overall condition, and something I noticed right away was that he was in very bad feather condition - he was missing his tail, and there was a huge section of primary feathers, on his left wing, which were missing; this would inhibit his flight, for sure. This was not a huge concern, because we could wait for the summer season and, with some good quality food and rest, this raven would moult out all of his broken feathers, ready for the next autumn.

Other than his feathers, he looked good. One thing I really underestimated, however, was that, unlike birds of prey, ravens can have psychological wounds - I would learn this in earnest, after I got him home!

"Okay, I'm very happy to take him," I said.

The breeder reassured me that five people had come to take a look at him, over the last two days, and none of them had seemed suitable.

He also confirmed that this bird had never been trained, and was kept in an aviary, so there was a lot of work to be done, in order to get him to fly free.

That's cool, I thought, as I always admire honesty. I don't know what he saw in me, but I was grateful and honoured that he considered me suitable for this raven's new home.

With a lot of effort, and a few colourful words from everyone, we finally managed to persuade the raven into a travel-box, and loaded him into the car. After a brief conversation with the breeder, about his favourite foods, and a look at his old raven baby pictures, we said our goodbyes and went back to the centre.

Upon arrival at the centre, we were greeted by most of the farm staff, who were eager to get a glimpse of this new addition to our flying team. I opened up the box, and the raven flew out, at an astronomical speed!

Once out, he appeared overwhelmed by the change of scenery; he was no longer in somebody's back garden - he was now in an orchard, with rolling hills in the background, and had no idea who the hell we were. He opened his beak, flattened his feathers, and looked utterly bewildered by the whole scene.

"I'm just going to sit with him on my own for a bit, as he looks a little freaked out," I called to everyone. So, they sat at a nearby table, while I held this giant corvid on my gloved hand.

Ravens have tiny eyes, considering the size of their heads – little, brown, beady things, which constantly observe.

He cocked his head to one side and furiously looked me up and down, trying to get some idea of my intentions. Suddenly, his head fluffed up again, and that familiar "Boh! Boh! Boh!" call was shouted at me.

After about ten minutes on my glove, he started to feel a little more comfortable, and this built up confidence in him, to abuse me a little more, physically - with every ounce of his being, the raven hammered his dagger-like beak into my leather glove. After each stabbing session, he then took great delight in seizing parts of the glove (with some fleshy parts of my hand included) in a vice-like grip, and twisting his head angrily, to try to maximize the pain for me, for absolutely no reason.

I had taken as much as I could bear - believe me: even in a leather gauntlet, designed to keep talons out, he was getting through, and it hurt! I tethered the little darling to a perch in his new aviary - quite frankly, until he got to know me, I did not fancy wrestling him and that beak. I put some quail down, for him to munch on. He did not touch the food. I locked up the aviary and let him be for the night.

"What on Earth have we done?" I said to my colleague; "That thing is wild... and bloody dangerous! His beak can literally take our eyes out, and he really isn't what I would call friendly."

My colleague looked back at me, with a worried smile; "I guess if he doesn't work out, we could always sell him on, as an aviary or breeding bird."

"Yeah, I guess," I replied; "I don't want to give up on him, but we can't have a dangerous bird here, at a public centre. Ah, we'll wait and see."

With that, we went home, where I was going to do some serious reading on the subject of raven behaviour.

Too many times in falconry, people will not admit when they don't have all the answers.

Ask most falconers, and they will have flown three of what you are enquiring about, and, of course, they will have done loop-the-loops and delivered speeches to the queen about your chosen subject!

Only a few times, in my life as a falconer, have I ever heard anyone say to me: "Do you know what? I don't actually know."

This gives rise to an almost self-defeating belief that you should know all the answers, but here is the truth: no-one does.

So, here I was: the only falconry centre in our area with a raven, with nobody nearby who had actually trained one. That's cool, I thought: I'll try to decipher the raven code – then, if we can understand each other better, I should be able to train him.

After returning home, I pulled up all the literature I could find on ravens in the wild, and in captivity - training methods, etc. - and began to piece together my own puzzle. I did not hand-rear this bird, because I had no idea what had happened to him in the first year of his life - all I knew was that he seemed frightened and aggressive; but, those two things go hand in hand: if I could make him trust me, we would be okay.

I listened to raven audio (very rock and roll), and picked out a few sounds which had been labelled as "friendly", by the scientists studying wild populations in their local area.

Ravens are incredibly intelligent - they have the same level of intelligence as a three-year old human child (and we all know how tenacious toddlers can be).

During their first two years of life, ravens form "gangs" of adolescent individuals, and it is at this point that they do their most damage - they are utter hooligans!

In teenage abandonment, the young ravens twist and turn in the air, and torment other species for no apparent reason, other than that they are there, and should therefore be the focus of their irritating games. They also learn to communicate with each other verbally - ravens make an astonishing array of sounds, to show exactly how they are feeling. They will even console their friends, if they have been targeted in an attack… and, boy, do these birds hold a grudge?

Very few species on this Earth have the ability or awareness to keep a vendetta going, but the raven is one of them.[8] They will dislike some individuals and like others - this goes for humans, in the hand-reared, captive-bred ravens, too.

As well as these mischievous episodes, ravens are capable of quite deep, positive emotions, and certainly exhibit signs of love, distress, uncertainty, trust, devotion, loyalty and cruelty - quite a mixed bag, for a bird.

Ravens have names in the wild, so he definitely needed a name, as he was a captive bird.

Mischief, trickery and a bird with a broken heart - I pondered this for a while; then, something came to me, which was perfect: Loki - he would be called Loki from now on.

The next day, I went in with Loki, and he still seemed pretty unsettled. He had not eaten since the night before, so I took out the old quail I had left him, and thought I would try an unconventional, but much-loved, treat: cookies! I had a choc-chip cookie to hand, and suddenly saw his eyes were very quizzical. I had read that ravens have a bit of a sweet beak, so a cookie might be just the job.

He jumped over to me and I broke off a piece of the biscuit, for him to try - gone! He took it out of my hand and hopped off with it, to take a closer look. After about one second, he had devoured the crumbs, and came back over, to take a look at what else I had. I now offered him pieces of the chick, and he took those quite readily, too.

"Okay, Loki," I uttered, "let's see if you're okay with the glove." I slid my gloved hand underneath him, and he grudgingly stepped up onto it.

Then, the naughty character came out of him, and I was hammered by his beak, once again. I put him down and turned my back on him.

Oh, he did not like that! He started cawing at me, harshly.

I turned back around to face him.

He slunk his head back, closer to his body, fluffed up his head and yelled at me: "Boh! Boh! Boh!" I had his attention now.

I threw a few more bits of food his way, and he quickly went about hoovering them up. Once again, I slid my glove towards him and he stepped up, this time without the hammering beak to accompany it. I stood up with him and he eyed me curiously.

Being that close to a beak, which was until this point being used as a weapon, is very daunting. But, I had to show that I trusted him, or else I would not be able to progress with the training. We stood there for about ten minutes, before I had the bright idea of trying to hand him food with my un-gloved right hand - big mistake!

My bare hand was the target this time, as Loki lunged forward, deliberately grabbing at my flesh. He twisted his beak from side to side, as if wanting to tear the flesh from my hand, and he almost succeeded - the power in his beak was phenomenal! He crushed the nerves between my thumb and fore-finger, until I could feel nothing other than pins and needles. As I tried to pull my poor, wounded hand away from his beak, the damage was made worse - he was not letting go; I had to bite the bullet, and ripped my hand away - he basically tore a scissor-cut, right through my thumb. The blood now pouring from me was a signal to end Day One.

I put Loki down, washed and bandaged my hand, and honestly thought about selling him, there and then - it was utterly heart-breaking. I gave him his rations of food for the day, which I just threw into the aviary - the good news was that he ate every last bit of it; the bad news was I hated him.

Throughout the first week, Loki lunged at my face, grabbed my glove, attacked my legs… He gave me wounds which would scar and last a lifetime. But, something else became clear: this bird also had scars.

Instead of trying to make him do things he did not want to do, I spent the next two weeks getting to know him. How did I know what he had been through? Had he bitten his previous owner and got a slap with a glove? Maybe that was why he hated the glove? To test that theory, I went in without a glove, and took a little pair of weighing scales into his aviary, which he now saw as his home - I put them on the big log, which lay on the floor of the aviary, and tried to tempt him up with some food.

"Come on, Loki," I said, in my most cheerful voice - ravens respond a lot to tone, and will do so accordingly if you shout at them, or have any kind of nervousness in your voice.

He hopped around the log for a bit, and then we had our breakthrough! He jumped onto the scales and sat there, with his beak open, ready for me to throw some food into it. In that moment, I could register his weight. We had a starting point, and no blood had been shed - a good day! I built on this, and spent more and more time in his aviary.

Loki started to call out to me, when I arrived at the centre - a very loud, shrieking: "Caw! Caw!"

I could tell, from the tone, that this meant he was excited to see me. I had his trust, I had not hurt him and every interaction with me was positive, and involved his favourite food.

I tried the glove again.

I picked him up and, to my surprise, there was no bad behaviour at all - he just sat there and started sounding a clicking, and a soothing tone. I carried him about, and he seemed to love looking around, outside his aviary, for the first time.

Ravens are not as strict, when it comes to flying weights - they do, of course, need to be keen, in order to react quickly to your commands, and not grow bored of you, but the trick of getting a raven to do what you want is down to whether or not they like and/or trust you.

Ravens bond incredibly closely with one or two individuals, and tend to aim disdain at others - this is probably due to the fact that they pair up for life and, once settled out of their hooligan stage, a pair will spend most of their lives together, even if they are part of a bigger flock.

This became apparent when anyone else tried to handle Loki - he would deliberately attack their Wellies or peck their clothing, because he just did not have the same respect for them; I am afraid to say that unless either myself or Elliot – my husband, who also works at Coda Falconry - are around, Loki will still try to terrorize the rest of my staff, to this day.

Elliot worked closely with Loki, in the early months, and built up an amazing rapport with him. He taught Loki how to play "Ker-plunk", how to fly to people's shoulders and how to play a specially designed xylophone - when he hit the right notes on the xylophone, Loki would be rewarded with his favourite treat (which we found out was cheese) and, because we were able to trust him, Loki became part of our flying demonstrations.

Loki's intelligence and eagerness to learn new things made him a joy to train, once the initial foundations had been laid - he went from a nasty, biting demon into a true friend, and when we took him off-site, on static demonstrations, Loki would prefer to sit on my lap, and "help" me to eat my sandwiches and drink my tea.

He flew freely around arenas in the UK, and around the farm, until one fateful demonstration where, despite our warnings before bringing Loki out - "do NOT eat food, as he WILL steal it" - a little girl decided to plonk out a jam doughnut, just after we had released Loki to do his demonstration. Loki clocked it before I did, strutted brazenly over to the girl and whipped the doughnut right out of her hands.

The audience thought it was hilarious, especially because he ate all of the jam out of the middle, then took the mushed-up dough back to the girl, in a sort of peace offering. However, it was a shot across the bows, that unless we can 100% guarantee that the audience will not interfere with his free flight, things could escalate and get nasty very quickly; not on the part of Loki, but just imagining if the parents of the girl had a fear of birds, it could have resulted in one of them striking out at Loki, and then we would be back to square one.

We therefore made the decision that when we take Loki off-site for his demonstration work, we should attach the creance to him, so that we can safely monitor what is going on, and he can be stopped if he shows a little moment of malicious intent.

People do love Loki - he has even been

invited to weddings! At our medieval shows,
Loki is the star and, because he trusts us, as
his handlers and guardians, he is very gentle on
the glove with our experience-day guests, as
long as we stand next to them, too.

We have actually just taught him to race -
after a countdown of "3... 2... 1... GO!", Loki will
race the lucky contender across our flying arena
(Loki always wins).

As I look back at how he has developed at
Coda Falconry, I must say that he is a bird of
which I am truly proud. I have never had to heal
a bird's broken heart and mind before; Loki's
complex behavioural patterns, vocalizations and
character meant that I really had to think outside
of the box, before we could even get him to like
us. Now that he does, he is excelling as a
working, well-rounded bird, which enjoys life,
once again.

He has opened up new worlds for me, too.
We were asked to do research, as part of a book
(which will probably be published before this one
ever is!), which seeks to understand raven
behaviour - as the author knew that Loki was a
very rare, trained working raven, he came to see
what he could do; I think it is safe to say that
Loki was a fascinating pupil.

As well as illustrating his movements, and
noting how he reacted with us, they requested
that we record some of his calls on an audio
recording device, as we had gone into detail
about his many strange and beautiful early
evening calls, and that they are unlike anything

wild ravens appear to do.

This is when we learnt, from the author, that ravens actually hear sounds in a much lower, slower frequency to us, and what we hear is completely different to that in a raven's world. As promised, we captured the whole array of sounds he likes to practice, when the public have gone home - as though he is trying out new vocals, with which to impress himself, and us, one day – and, apparently there was a noise in there, which mimicked my laugh. But I am having none of it! Well, unless I really do sound like an evil genius at times.

After a confusing, stressful start to his life, Loki had come to us with no idea of what might happen next, and this fear manifested itself in aggressive behaviour.

By accepting that Loki was, at his core, a frightened little boy, it became so much easier to forgive him each painful bite - he was only acting on instincts, which told him: "I don't like this, because I don't understand what is going on, or what you are going to do to me".

I am so pleased that we decided to persevere with him, and get the best out of his inquisitive character. As soon as Loki learnt that we were not going to hurt him, and that we were offering him not only a safe-haven, to call home, but an opportunity to roam around, freely, across the farm, he mellowed, then actually started to seek out our company.

I have learnt a lot from Loki.

For example, I found out that ravens are exceptionally jealous creatures - if Loki sees me flying any of the other birds in the centre, he will angrily call to me, until I am back outside his aviary; then, his manners return to him, and he goes back to his usual bubbling clicks and tones, which tell me that he is very happy to see me, and that he honestly thought I was never coming back to him!

A complex character - it took a long time to realize where Loki was coming from, and a lot of love to bring him around.

After being taken from a place he had got to know well, Loki had formed an opinion on humans, and what he could get from life, before we met him. After showing him a new set of possibilities and using positive, food-based reward, to test his mind and stretch his wings, it was like a whole new colour palate had been added to his life, and he had so much more to look forward to than just sitting in an aviary, alone.

Loki is now three-years old, and I can appreciate him more now, and what he went through. I saw him as a beast, who was ready to hurt me at any given time - I did not understand what he was trying to achieve, or what he wanted from me; I was frustrated that he did not understand me.

It is when I realize that Loki felt exactly the same about me, in those early days, that I fully appreciate the depth of his mind, and the amazing feeling that being loved by a raven can give you.

EPILOGUE

Coda Falconry is now thriving, it has won two awards: "Best New Business (Business Excellence awards 2013)" and "Best Customer Service (Best Women Business Awards 2016)".

I also represent the NatWest "Women in Business" programme, where my story has been told to try and encourage women to start up their own businesses.

One of the reasons I continued Coda Falconry in the face of adversity, was to make my family proud. And it was only after much persuasion from my long-suffering mum that I decided to finally write this book.

I really hope that you have enjoyed learning, not only about falconry as a sport, but also about the tight bond required between a human and a bird of prey, for it to be done well. It has been a pleasure to share some of my knowledge and passion with you.

I believe that falconry should be taught on a mass level, to a wider demographic – perhaps, one day, falconry will become a more mainstream sport. Hard work, diligence, training and respect - these are the key elements of falconry.

It is strange for me to hear people saying anything negative about falconry as the birds in a good falconer's care will never know hunger, illness, cold, parasites or pain. They enjoy the skies - we give them their realm and they can spend as long as they like up there with the added bonus of knowing that when they want to return and have their food, they can. Human beings also benefit from having such a close bond with an aloof creature and learn patience, tolerance and the true language of nature.

Birds of prey used to be integral to our survival and happiness. That partnership still exists but it's hanging on by a thread and it needs people with fresh ideas to love the sport again.

Do you love birds of prey?

Are you able to perceive nature in a different way to that which you have been taught, and are you willing to open your heart, to a friendship which will make a mark on your soul, forever?

When you stand alone with your newly-trained raptor, for the first time, the world around you will feel different - your perspective will change, and you will start listening to the alarm calls of other birds, and the direction the wind is blowing in.

When she opens her wings, looks around at her surroundings and pushes off from your glove, as you let go of her flying jesses, she takes her first flight into her element, and a part of you will go with her. When she returns to your glove, after her flight, and nestles into you, after eating her fill of food, that is her way of saying:

"Take me home, please."
And, you will be so glad to oblige…
She flew away, but then she came back, out of choice.

This is the freedom of falconry.

REFERENCES:

1. Ancient & Medieval Falconry: Origins & Functions in Medieval England by Shawn E. Carroll
2. Birdlife International Data Zone 2017
3. The Nature Conservancy - Journey with Nature "Peregrine Falcons"
4. Sexing Barn Owls - The Barn Owl Trust
5. "The Sunda Scops Owl" www.planetofbirds.com
6. Alzheimer's Society, UK
7. The Eagle Owl in Britain Tim Melling, Steve Dudley and Paul Doherty
8. Live Science - Crows Hold Grudges in Humanlike Fashion

AUTHOR'S ACKNOWLEDGEMENTS

The staff and volunteers at Coda Falconry are the heart and soul of the centre.

When I look at how much they have progressed along their own falconry journey within the company over the years, I feel overwhelmingly proud of them all.

My longest employed staff member, Emily Corless is an outstanding example of what can be achieved if people are inspired by doing something that they love. Emily started working with me at the age of 14 years old and is now the head falconer at Coda Falconry 6 years on. I have never, in my whole life, met a more dedicated and able falconer – she is the promise of things to come and a great reflection on how the younger generations can change and adapt falconry for the better.

Without my friends and family, none of my dreams would have come to fruition. Their support and loyalty to me is something that I cannot quantify – it's the reason I carry on doing what I do.

Of all the members of my family, it's my mum who has had to put up with the most. Sharing her life with my birds wasn't natural or easy for her but she believed in my dream and confronted any situation I found myself in with words of wisdom, honesty and dignity.

As she has been by my side for the whole journey of Coda Falconry, I thought it was only right that she penned her side of the story.

ABOUT THE AUTHOR

(As described by her mother)

From an early age, Sarah-Jane has had a love for birds and would often arrive home carrying various birds found stunned or injured that needed care. I must admit I didn't share her enthusiasm but whether it took a few hours, or a day or so, they were all released after being fed and rested, to continue life on the wing. So it's no surprise that she felt drawn to work with birds and after a course of study, took a brave decision to establish a falconry centre in an urban area. From small beginnings, many an adventure and drama later, her centre for falconry is an opportunity to view birds close up, as well as in flight.

Like any new undertaking it's been hard-won, with a lot of dedication, heartbreaks and disappointments. Flying birds is the tip of the iceberg. The daily routine that's evolved over the years is a programme of weighing, feeding and flying birds, cleaning enclosures, and in the process getting to know the character and foibles of each bird. Who knew birds have likes and dislikes? It seems to me that birds of a feather may fly together but are in fact a complex group of individuals.

Learning best practice both from falconry traditions as well as her own experience, Sarah's main concern is always for the welfare, safety and well-being of each bird. The result of this is a community of birds well at ease with their surroundings. In writing down and sharing the lessons learnt, Sarah's notes offer a source of fresh and invaluable advice for anyone considering keeping a bird of prey, or who may just have an interest in knowing more about these creatures.

Inevitably, obstacles of working with any animal has to be overcome daily, and there has been many a mini-adventure, including the astounding sight of seeing Sarah fetch and climb a ladder to rescue an owl, refusing to fly down from a tree!

Small they may be, but birds have exacting needs; they also watch, and take note of more than might be realised. In return they deserve observant and responsive care. Sarah's love, knowledge and experience of falconry is very evident and generously shared with anyone interested in learning more, and although unashamedly biased, I am very proud of my daughter

ABOUT THE PUBLISHER

L.R. Price Publications is dedicated to publishing books by unknown authors.

We use a mixture of both traditional and modern publishing options to bring our authors' words to the wider world.

We print, publish, distribute and market books in a variety of formats including paper and hard back, e-books, digital audio books and online.

If you're an author interested in getting your book published; or a book retailer interested in selling our books, please contact us.

www.lrpricepublications.com

L.R. Price Publications Ltd,

27 Old Gloucester Street,

London, WC1N 3AX.

020 3051 9572

publishing@lrprice.com

Printed in Great Britain
by Amazon

84662291R00090